THE KINGDOM OF GOD

VOLUME THREE

LEARNING WAR NO MORE

TOM A. JONES

The Kingdom of God—Volume Three
Learning War No More

© 2020 by Tom A. Jones

All rights reserved.
No part of this book may be duplicated, copied, translated, reproduced or stored mechanically or electronicly without specific, written permission of Illumination Publishers International.

All Scripture quotations, unless otherwise indicated, are taken from the THE HOLY BIBLE, NEW INTERNATIONAL VERSION®, NIV® Copyright © 1973, 1978, 1984, 2011 by Biblica, Inc.® Used by permission. All rights reserved worldwide.

Printed in the United States of America

Cover Design: Brian Branch

ISBN: 978-1-948450-82-9

www.ipibooks.com

CONTENTS

Preface 5

Introduction 9

Chapter 1 – Thank You for Your Service 18

Chapter 2 – Man's Wisdom or God's? 27

Chapter 3 – The Prince of Peace: He Is Coming 40

Chapter 4 – The Prince of Peace: He Has Come 49

Chapter 5 – The Teaching of the Early Church 60

Chapter 6 – Just War Theory 74

Chapter 7 – The Military Experience 92

Chapter 8 – Good Questions 114

Chapter 9 – Better Questions 133

Chapter 10 – The Toughest Question 151

Chapter 11 – Practical Particulars 164

Chapter 12 – A "Disputable" Matter? 171

Chapter 13 – Summing Up 178

Chapter 14 – Mind Change… "But God" 181

☙

Appendix – Kingdom Love for Enemies 189

End Notes 198

Bibliography 205

DEDICATIONS

To Ray Dean Gregory, who returned to Jesus and his church not long ago. He walked with me the last two years of his life and was taken from us with shocking suddenness, but inspired me with his smile and joy to his last day here. To use his favorite word: Absolutely!

To Jon Hazelip, who suddenly appeared in my life when he was seventy-eight, and was just as quickly gone soon after he turned seventy-nine. In six months with him, I came to know well his love for Jesus and the Kingdom of God. I am grateful for the remarkable impact he made on my life.

And, finally, to Wyndham Shaw, my friend of forty-seven years. He personally encouraged me for more than thirty years as I faced the challenge of MS. Then I watched him courageously and faithfully deal with multiple systems atrophy, an even more devasting disease. He was seeking the Kingdom first all the way to the end.

We lost all these in 2019. They were dear friends. I look forward to a sweet reunion.

PREFACE

The book you are reading is not the one that was envisioned five years ago. And it is not the one envisioned two years ago, nor the one envisioned even eight or nine months ago. The proverb is true: "In their hearts humans plan their course, but the Lord establishes their steps" (Proverbs 16:9).

We began nine years ago with plans for a three-volume work on the vital topic of the Kingdom of God. We had, and still have, a passion for speaking and writing on this crucial message of Jesus. Some of you will remember that after Volume One was published, Volume Two followed the next year. So, it was not long before we heard from many readers who were awaiting the final installment. Eventually, it was outlined and topics assigned. Deadlines were set up. Some work was completed, but then life (or the Spirit), intervened again, and again.

My coauthor and good friend, Steve Brown, found himself involved deeply in crucial ministry situations where his knowledge of Scripture, Latin American culture, and church missions, not to mention his mastery of Spanish, were all greatly needed. Increasingly, it became clear that finishing what the two of us began several years ago was going to fall to me.

At first, I decided to tackle all the topics we had originally envisioned, but then even that plan had to be put aside. While disappointed to a certain extent, I was not ready to give up on the project entirely. Maybe it was because biblically "3" seems to be a better number than "2." More than likely, it was because we had made a commitment, but something was unfinished.

In due course, my focus narrowed. Feeling there was a major topic so central to kingdom thinking that it needed to be addressed, I decided to complete a more modest project. I made this decision with the faith that if this were not the best, God could easily dash this plan, too. For a while, I thought maybe he was doing just that. But, alas, a rush of inspiration returned along with continued encouragement from others to write.

That you are holding this book in your hand in some form, paper or electronic, means that I was finally able to see this much-revised plan through to completion. Paul did say, "We must go through many hardships to enter the kingdom of God." Why should we expect less even to write about it and proclaim it?

So, here is what you will finally find in this book: a kingdom perspective on something deeply embedded into human affairs throughout the world—enemies, soldiering, war, and the military; and the Kingdom of God's relationship to all those.

I must emphasize one thing: this work represents my thoughts and ideas. Unlike the first two volumes, this one is not coauthored. If you find problems here, do not blame my friend Steve. You can go after both of us for the first two volumes. With this one, just blame me. Steve is not responsible. Because he is a trusted friend, he was most certainly one of the people I sought input from. This has not gone to press without his reading it and giving me his thoughts. But in the end, Steve and more than a dozen other friends who provided counsel will not be responsible for the content. I will. Writing is always helped and strengthened by the review and comments of others, and I am very grateful for all the feedback I received, but if there are still mistakes or a failure to present the most Kingdom-oriented material with the right tone, that will be my doing.

(By the way, as Steve and I discussed this revamping of Volume

Three, he expressed the hope that we might still at some point return to some of our original thinking and do what could become a Volume Four. This we will entrust to God in prayer. But no promises! And no emails from you, please! If it doesn't happen, I have assured myself that I will have no feelings of something unfinished.).

That being said, on subject after subject, topic after topic, we need to return to the concept of the Kingdom. I recently heard the gifted teacher, Michael Burns, teaching on "Culture, Race, and Kingdom," and in my home congregation he made this statement: "I know here in Nashville, you have heard a lot of teaching on the Kingdom, but I also know this: *You have not heard enough!*" He is so right. There is much to say about the message of the Kingdom of God that was the heart of Jesus' teaching. With these three volumes, Steve and I have just scratched the surface. Maybe we have told you almost all we know, but that just means we have much more to learn. Prayerfully, we have helped you see how central the Kingdom is to everything about Jesus, given you a more biblical way to think about it, and stirred you to keep seeking it first the rest of your life.

This book focuses on the issue of nonviolence, peacemaking, and enemy-love, but it is Volume Three in a series about the *nature and character of the Kingdom.* It highlights an idea we have emphasized from the beginning: the message of the Kingdom is not so much about going to heaven when you die, but about living heaven (or eternal life, especially in John's Gospel) on earth now, before the great consummation of all things. The Kingdom is about "the now" and "the not yet." The not yet is real and coming, but we are first called to show the nature of it right now.

As you work out your thinking on this subject I will address, evaluate your starting point. If you didn't start with the Kingdom, you need a do-over. Don't start with hypothetical situations and "what-ifs" or even with actual events, using the world's wisdom and reason to draw a conclusion. Start, instead, with the upside-down nature of the Kingdom and follow it even when it leads to upside-down conclusions, like dying on a cross for other people. Remember: First, the Kingdom! Keep asking, "Does my conclusion fit with the nature of the Kingdom, the ethos of the Kingdom, the attitudes of the Kingdom?" (Matthew 5:3–11).

INTRODUCTION
LEARNING WAR NO MORE

While I have been encouraged by some to write about the disciple of Jesus, enemies, war, and the military, I know that many will wonder why this topic at this time. Surely there are a dozen topics more relevant and pressing than this one. What about the Kingdom and race relations? Yes, that is an absolutely crucial one and, for sure, a timely one. But others like Michael Burns and my good friend Gordon Ferguson are doing excellent work addressing it. (And, by the way, I did manage to include Appendix 2, which is a very personal perspective on race by someone you can call "Alabama Tom Jones." Also, there is Appendix 3 by my bride of fifty years on the same subject.)

But back to the topic of this book, we might ask: Are that many people asking questions about it? Is there a hot debate? Are people hungry for answers? The answer is most certainly no. However, I hope before I am done, you will see that this matter is far more central to our lives as disciples of Jesus than you may at first think. Maybe you will find that one author was not going too far when he said that *this subject is at the essence of the gospel.* Perhaps you will find, as have I, that wrestling with this issue will take your faith and your understanding of the Kingdom to a new level.

Right now, in the fellowship of churches where I seek to live out my faith, there is much discussion about the role of women. I am wholeheartedly behind any effort for us to reexamine our traditional understanding of this matter. We are not being faithful, and probably will not be fruitful, if we are limiting God's plan for our sisters to serve and lead in the Kingdom. But that topic has our attention, while the subject of this book does not. I hope I can help change that. I don't want to diminish interest in the one, but encourage interest in the other. They are both vitally related to all Jesus meant when he said, "the Kingdom."

In Volume One of this series we started with the indisputable but often overlooked fact that the Kingdom of God was Jesus' main message. We then saw that when Jesus spoke of the Kingdom, he was referring to the age to come breaking into the present age (see figure 1). The Kingdom first broke in with Jesus himself and continues to come in the lives of those who follow him and whose citizenship is in heaven. They live in response to heaven's will in the midst of a world that has other standards, pressures, and requirements.

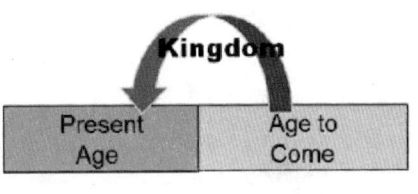

Figure 1

At the heart of this life is every word in this essential prayer: "Your kingdom come, your will be done, on earth as it is in heaven." This means the goal of the follower of Jesus is not just "to go to heaven when you die" but "to live heaven and its principles here and now on earth before you die." Jesus shows us life as it should be, and he redeems those who follow him from an empty way of life that goes in mostly wrong directions. He sets our feet on a new path, one that is so different that it enables us to bring light into the darkness, but often causes those who embrace the light to be seen as foreigners and aliens.

In Volume Two we examined closely Jesus' teaching in what is called the Sermon on the Mount. In our view, this could more appropriately be called the Sermon on the Kingdom, describing not the location from which it was given but the subject it explored. From the beginning, where Jesus describes the essential attitudes of the kingdom life (what we call the Beatitudes) to the middle, where he urges us to seek the Kingdom first, to the end, where he describes those who will be and will not be in the Kingdom, Jesus gives us a rather detailed and uncompromising picture of what it means to live out the Kingdom in this present age.

In Chapter 17 of Volume Two, we looked at what Jesus taught as the kingdom posture toward enemies, those who oppose you and want to harm you. There you will find the foundation for what I will say in this book. If you want to review that after you finish this introduction, and you don't have a copy of Volume Two handy, you will find it as Appendix 1 in this volume. You may find a quick review of those thoughts to be helpful. If you have not read that chapter from Volume Two, I would urge you to go there before starting Chapter 1.

It is as remarkable as it is disturbing, how widely Jesus' basic instructions in his Sermon on the Mount have been dismissed, ignored, and avoided even by those who want to wear his name. However, if the followers of Jesus are to really be his disciples, we must get back to this core teaching and make it the center of our lives. If we are to "teach them to obey everything I have commanded you," this must be our starting point.

Since kingdom living requires that we rethink our view of

everything from righteousness to relationships to sex to money, it should follow that it would cause us to rethink our view of enemies, the military, and war. After all, this is often a matter of life and death, not to mention being such a fact of life. Jesus was a revolutionary messiah and teacher. It would be surprising if his message didn't also turn our thinking upside down in this area.

This is a vital area for Christian exploration and discussion, but I believe we have virtually ignored it. *I strongly suspect that for many of you this will be the first book you have ever read that deals with the disciple, the military, and war.* Yet we have Christians who are in the military, and from time to time I hear of more who are enlisting. In some countries (twenty-six at last count) a period of military service is mandatory. Is this a situation in which to just comply, or is it one in which to think, "We must obey God rather than men"?

Of course, not everyone lands where I do on this topic. Some of them have never thought seriously about the issues. I have had committed disciples tell me they just haven't considered it. Others have done so and have reasons for their position. In this book, I will attempt to be fair and tell you how they think, but I want to make sure that at least once, you have heard someone make (or try to make) a clear case for what we might correctly call *Christian pacifism*—the decision of disciples of Jesus, because they follow him, to not be involved in the killing of enemies, but instead to be committed to a lifestyle of enemy-love and peacemaking.[1]

Yes, I used that term pacifism, though in doing so there is some risk. At times, I have not liked the word, and no doubt, some of you have negative feelings when you hear it. In the past, I confused it with what we might call "passivism." However, one of the main synonyms for the correct word "pacifism" is "peacemaking." That is just what Jesus called us to (Matthew 5:9), and when properly understood, we see that pacifism (active peacemaking) is far from being passive. God is in the reconciling business, and those who go about the ministry of reconciliation may start by refusing to take the lives of others, but that is just the beginning. They are active not passive, reaching out in love to those who oppose them or want to harm them.

By the way, I will not be presenting pacifism as an idea that is guaranteed to "always work," if we mean that it always has a nice outcome for the pacifist and for the aggressor. I will not offer any assurances about where it may lead, except to a closer following of Jesus and the opportunity to share in his suffering love.

Regardless of the way we approach this subject, for many Christians, this is a hard teaching. I speak as an American when I say we live in a culture, for the most part, that celebrates the military. Many of us just do it instinctively. We know many wonderful people who are in the military. We hear some great stories of heroism. We know disciples of Jesus with great hearts that are in the military. A friend of mine who graduated from the Naval Academy and was a Navy pilot for six years was a pre-pub reader of this book. Among the notes he wrote me was this:

> Christians in the Western world are free to practice their faith, to worship God in many diverse ways, and do not fear the persecution that is practiced in other parts of the world. If the Western countries eliminated their military forces, the worldly expectation is that the safety and security of the citizens would quickly be lost. We revere and honor the military because of what they do to secure that safety for us all. And yet what they do is truly violent, and is fully intended to be violent. This is the hardest moral dilemma we face in choosing to be Christ-like in non-violence.

While most people I know are no warmongers, we honor and hold up "those who fight for and guard our freedom." On the night I first was working on this project, I saw the following on an NFL team website:

> Before the game, the Chargers kicked off their 28th annual "Salute to the Military" with 240 military members presenting a "super flag" and color guards from each of the four major military branches presenting the regular-sized flag.[2]

Political parties may disagree about many things, sometimes in disgusting fashion, but they usually agree on an event like this that honors and supports men and women in uniform. When there are those who question whether the military is the place for a kingdom man or woman, they may be suspected of ingratitude or something even more dangerous.

Because this can be a very emotional topic, I know at any point in this book, I may lose some of you. Before that happens, let me be clear about several matters:

1. I do not intend to villainize the military. I see many strong points in military service and in those who serve and will devote the first chapter of this book to that matter. But I want you to know that I did not write that chapter as a psychological device to "soften" someone up. It is sincerely stated. Many, if not most of you, will agree with what I say there, and, ironically, for that very reason, it will be hard for some of you to hear some of the other things I will say.

2. I will not write that soldiering (or policing) is evil or sinful, the

way stealing or lying are sinful. But I will attempt a number of times to show that once we are in the Kingdom, as citizens of heaven, *this is not a role that God intends for us to fulfill in the world* because there are actions involved in this role that are at odds with our kingdom calling. On the one hand, if Jesus is not the Christ of God, the position of Christian pacifism taken in this book is foolish, idiotic, and insane. However, since he is the Christ, then this may very well be another of God's upside-down ways of showing his Kingdom and its nature to the world.

3. I do not want to try to push you into a certain conclusion. When I heard from a trusted early reader of this book that I had ultimately persuaded her, but it would have been much better if she was made to feel that I was giving her more room to come to her own conclusion, I knew changes had to be made. I hope the present copy represents those changes. John D. Roth is surely correct when he writes, "Arguments for Christian pacifism that seek to win their case through rhetorical bluster or crafty forms of logical manipulation have missed the whole point. At its very essence, Christian faith is invitational rather than coercive."[3] I long to see Christians come together in unity, but that can happen only through a noncontrolling love. Please forgive me if I ever seem to stray from that goal.

4. I believe that Jesus' teaching about an astonishing love for enemies and about nonviolence are core issues that must not be ignored, but this does not mean I will question the reality of your faith or, God forbid, your salvation, if you do not agree with me on what those teachings mean. If at any point you feel I could not enjoy fellowship with you as my Christian sister or my Christian brother, please know that no disagreement on this topic would

cause me to feel that way, or at least, cause me to give in to those feelings. I will say more about this later in Chapter 12.

I trust you, my readers. If you have come to this point in this series in seeking the Kingdom of God, I believe that you are probably among the "Kingdom few," those rare people God is looking for, and you will not easily discard this before giving it a fair hearing.

If you ever decide to stop reading, I have one request: Before you go, please skip over and read Chapter 14, the last chapter, a shorter one titled "Mind Change: '…But God.'" I want you to know me, not just on the outside, but on the inside, and how I personally got to this point.

Let me close this introduction with several brief comments:

1. As we go along, many of you will raise questions. Before we are done, I will try to anticipate and answer as many of those as possible (in Chapters 8 through 12). You may want to write me about those I don't address. You may help me to see truth I have overlooked or resisted myself. At any rate, I am grateful you have chosen to travel with me a little further down this road of kingdom exploration.

2. Just as I was about to send this book off to the publisher, I got back some late comments from one of my early readers. His thoughts were a good reminder to me that everyone who reads this book will bring an abundance of personal and varied experience to the engagement of the ideas presented here. For a few minutes that was an overwhelming thought, but it is one that is always true. My prayer just has to be: let the truth of Jesus come

through all the different filters. (And I hope you pray that it will come through all of yours!)

3. Please understand that in very many ways, this is an aspirational book. I have convictions I believe need to be shared, but I do not claim to have arrived. So much I will write about is a challenge to me, but I must not wait until I achieve all I aspire to. Indeed, everything we say or write about the Kingdom of God should bring us back to the first beatitude, the first principle of kingdom life, where we say, "God be merciful, for I am most certainly spiritually poor." I want to continue this prayer, with the hope that you can join me in saying:

Father, guide us as we seek to understand that Jesus is the Prince of Peace, that he called us to be peacemakers and that he teaches us to love our enemies. Show us, Father, how to do that. You have promised that if we keep on seeking, we will find. We want to please you. We want to show your Kingdom breaking into this world. May it come individually and collectively. May your will be done on earth, now in our lives, as it is in heaven.

1
THANK YOU FOR YOUR SERVICE

I have told you that I am convinced that Christian pacifism represents a kingdom perspective, so it may seem odd where I want to go in this chapter. However, I think it most important to start with what is good about the military and why it is so often held in high esteem. In a book like this, leaving that out would simply not be fair.

Rare is the country on Planet Earth that does not love its military and does not give support to its troops. Crowds in most all countries are stirred by the sight of their nation's military on parade. Smart uniforms, bodies moving in unison, flags unfurled, drums and bugles sounding off—hearts are moved, eyes grow moist. In these moments we are proud to be British or American or Russian. We feel pride at being Canadian, Japanese, Nigerian or Pakistani or Brazilian or South African. You fill in the blank. Somehow the military men and women of our nation embody our values and symbolize our unity.

Dr. Gordon S Livingston writing in *Psychology Today* magazine says, "No idea in the society is more pervasive than the notion that we all owe a debt of gratitude to the young men and women who have volunteered to fight our wars."[4]

The troops represent the nation, serve the nation, and put themselves in harm's way for the nation. It has been said that no group understands better the idea of putting your country above yourself than those in the military. In most cases their presence gives their compatriots a sense of security. It is no wonder that people often say, "Thank you for your service." Again, I quote my friend, the former Navy pilot:

> My experience with military people is that the vast majority of them do what they do in the true sense of service to their country. They do not want war. They do not wish to fight. The best military life they wish for is that their presence acts as a deterrent to war, such that they never have to actually use the terrible skills they have been trained to use. Military people, just like the populace, also want peace—but the difference is that they are willing to put their lives on the line if it becomes necessary. "Greater love has no one than this, that a man lay down his life for his friends." This is indeed what military people are willing to do. "Thanks for your service" is an honor for that willingness.

This appreciation for the military is by no means limited to those with a secular worldview. While such support is found through all strata of our society, no segment of the United States is more supportive of the armed forces than those who are part of Bible-believing evangelical churches. It is common to see signs in front of houses of worship that read "Support our troops" or "Pray for our troops." In polling every year, Congress gets an approval rating of 15% or lower, while the military consistently scores around 85%, with even higher ratings from evangelical Christians. A respected Christian website that answers questions submitted by readers responds to a question about the military this way: "At the same time, Christians can rest assured that being a soldier is highly respected throughout the Scriptures and know that such service is consistent with a biblical worldview." Later it concludes: "The Christian men and women who serve their country with character, dignity, and honor can rest assured that the civic duty they perform is condoned and respected by our sovereign God. Those who honorably serve in the military deserve our respect and gratitude."[5]

In searching the web for the connection between churches and troop-support efforts, I did not find much of an effort to show a biblical basis for such support, but did find numerous sites giving church members ideas of how to support men and women in uniform. One might think that Scripture says that true religion is found in caring for widows, orphans, and the troops.

Offering Protection

For Americans and, I suspect, for others, the number one reason for supporting our troops is that they are seen as those that risk their lives to guard our freedoms and provide protection. Again, Dr. Livingstone writes: "All our wars, of course, are justified as struggles for freedom, either our own or that of the people in the countries in which we fight." In the words of British politician and former cabinet minister, Des Browne, "We have a responsibility to support our troops and support their families, particularly when we are asking people to do very difficult and dangerous things for our security."[6]

On the other hand, we should add that while many give thanks for troops that protect their freedoms, in some totalitarian countries and in those with strong dictatorships, troops maintain order but with harsh tactics, and they also prevent people from exercising freedoms that they yearn for. Instead of protecting freedom, they are experts at suppressing it. However, even in these countries, the propaganda machine is usually successful in focusing the nation on their enemies and in keeping their people appreciating their troops.

It is likely that some reader of this book will want to remind me that I have the freedom to write this material because the armed forces of my country protect that freedom. I understand why someone might connect those dots for an American like me, but I would have to remind them that the military can just as easily be used to suppress freedom as to guarantee it. In truth many of the writings of Christians through the centuries have been done under governments who sought to suppress them, and I would insist that even when governments or armies cannot guarantee our freedom that God finds a way to get his truth out regardless.

While there are two sides of the military coin, still, in most people's minds, the top reason to appreciate the military is the protection and security it usually offers in a world with many bad actors. But there are other reasons to appreciate its work.

Rendering Aid

When natural disasters strike, the military is often more capable of responding that any other segment of society. They have the person-power, the equipment, the organization, the readiness and the efficiency to offer big doses of help to local emergency responders. Sometimes they can do what no one else can do. Witness the helicopter rescues in New Orleans in 2005 and Houston in 2017, after devastating floods that followed hurricanes. Following the October 2005 earthquake in Pakistan, it was the combined effort of the armies of many countries that provided the largest humanitarian helicopter airlift ever seen.

On September 20, 2017, Hurricane Maria destroyed much of the island of Puerto Rico. Three weeks later the U.S. general in charge of the military response would report that they had 68 helicopters and 14,300 troops aiding the recovery. While much remains to be done, even as I write this, there is no doubt that the military made a big difference.

On the U.S. Army website, army.mil, you can find a special section titled "Humanitarian Relief." A recent check of that page revealed their efforts to restore power and put on roofs in Puerto Rico, help with pediatric nutrition in Honduras, and provide aid to burned-out victims during the California wildfires. On the website one reads: "Providing humanitarian relief in the United States and around the world is an essential part of the mission of the U.S. Army." Having the military at the ready when disaster creates a crisis would certainly be seen as a plus by people of various nations who have come to count on their own armed forces at such times.

Inspiring Others

Most of us will not be in circumstances where we are asked to risk our lives for the good of another, but those in the military are often operating in a sphere where that is exactly what they have the opportunity to do. And it is from that sphere that we hear some of the most heart-moving stories of these qualities on display.

Author Mark Lee Greenblatt reached out to interview quite a few members of the military who had demonstrated great heroism before writing his most recent book. One of these was an enlisted Marine named James Hassell. His platoon was in a firefight in Najaf, Iraq. His friend, Ryan, took a hit and was badly wounded. Knowing his buddy would die if he left him there, James decided to pick him up and carry him to the medivac helicopter that was at the end of an alley a hundred yards away. It was a high-risk move; together they would present a slow-moving target with snipers everywhere. But it was Ryan's only chance, and James decided to risk his own life to give him that chance. They made it. Ryan is alive today.[7] On his website,

Greenblatt describes many other heroic acts[8] and wrote a profound article on courage for the military.com website.[9]

When I read of the James Hassels of the world and stories of winners of the Victoria Cross, the Silver Star, the Congressional Medal of Honor, or the Legion of Honor, I am humbled by the bravery and sacrifice these people have shown. Since I know that other civilians are also affected as I am through seeing what is done by military people, it is reasonable to say these qualities, to some extent, affect the entire populace.

Additional Value for Military Members

The first two items we have put in the positive column for the military are activities appreciated from those even on the outside. Some of the other positives that are often listed may be most appreciated by those on the inside. Let's consider a few.

1. Providing valuable training

When one enters the military of any country that person receives basic training regardless of the role they will eventually fulfill. Very often some of the focus is on developing character. According to the U.S. Army, the leadership seeks to inculcate seven basic values in every soldier:

1. Loyalty
2. Duty
3. Respect
4. Selfless service
5. Honor
6. Integrity
7. Personal courage

A similar list of virtues or values can be found for the U.S. Navy, the British Royal Navy, and other fighting forces throughout the world. To you, these may seem to be traits for everyone to aspire to, but the military sees them as essential if they are to fulfill their mission. There are plenty who report that it was in the military that they learned some of their most important life lessons: to overcome fear, to take responsibility, to respect the importance of leadership, to appreciate accountability, and to be willing to sacrifice for others.

Beyond the seven basic values, those in the military are given skills they can use outside their military careers. There are the various technical fields of electronics, environmental science, robotics, aviation, navigation, and the like. For those eager to learn, there are ample opportunities to grow in leadership ability, planning, strategic thinking, team building, and other skills that may greatly help them later on in business, education, or even humanitarian work.

2. *Giving one a sense of purpose*

While working on this chapter, I stopped to watch a little of a talk show on one of the cable news networks. The host introduced his four guests, including one who was a former military officer. He looked to be between thirty-five and forty years old. He still had his soldier's haircut. He wore a navy blazer. Eventually the camera pulled back showing the entire group. It was then that I saw that the former officer had two prosthetic legs. I stayed longer than I first intended and eventually heard him describe his career as one motivated by a desire to serve something greater than himself.

Listening to him, I was painfully reminded of something I once said in a rather heated discussion with some other Christian teachers. My foolish comment went this way: "The values of the military are the exact opposite of the values of the Kingdom." Several roundly criticized my statement, and I understand why. It was an overstatement and a half truth. Both the Kingdom of God and the military do exactly what that disabled warrior said: they call for followers to serve something greater than themselves. The overlap of kingdom principles and military values does not stop there, but I won't explore it fully here. Suffice it to say, while there are also some big differences in the two (which we will explore in Chapter 7), they are alike in calling us to sacrifice for a higher or greater purpose. As one soldier put it, "That's when you learn the true meaning of service."

3. Developing deeper relationships

Many military veterans talk often about the way they learned to appreciate others, rely on others, and be devoted to the good of others during their time of service. A good number of those who leave the military talk of how they miss the comradery they enjoyed. They talk of the team spirit they developed and what it meant to be in a group where there was deep loyalty to one another.

Journalist Sebastian Junger, famously known as the author of *The Perfect Storm,* spent fourteen months embedded with a platoon in Afghanistan and then wrote the simply titled, *War.* One of his major points is how combat gives soldiers an intense experience of connection with one another and the way many of them miss war when they are no longer in it. But as Junger explains in a TED talk, it is not the killing that they miss or the experience of being shot at, but it is the brotherhood.[10]

Of course, not every military person ends up in combat, but even those who do not often report that in working together with others for a greater cause, they found deeper relationships than they had known before.

Then, too, there is the fact that the military can bring together people from diverse backgrounds, teaching them to build relationships that transcend the normal borders of race and culture and even gender (though, clearly, this one is a work in progress). It is in the armed forces that many have learned what M.L. King spoke about: the content of a person's character matters far more than the color of their skin or some other external.

※

I think I understand why the military has such a high approval rating and is treated with so much respect both in my country and in others. Without a doubt, there are good reasons why so many think highly of the women and men in uniform. As I was making some final edits to this book, the world celebrated the seventy-fifth anniversary of D-Day. By way of TV and the internet, millions were touched by the scenes of ninety-five-year-old veterans, mostly using canes or wheelchairs, coming to Normandy, likely one last time. They gathered at military cemeteries where thousands are buried to remember the event that began the liberation of Europe. Some of you have family who are proud veterans. Some of you are proud veterans. Some of you are on active duty right now. Some may even be deployed in an active war zone. I do not lightly dismiss the service of those in the military.

I think I can imagine what you feel when you hear me say, let's consider another way or let's ask if this is the role for a citizen of the Kingdom. But as those in the military teach us, we must always respond to a higher calling. With God's help, that is what we will seek to do.

2
MAN'S WISDOM OR GOD'S?

The term "paradigm shift" was first introduced in 1962 by American physicist and philosopher Thomas Kuhn in his book, *The Structure of Scientific Revolutions*. Eventually his concept was applied to many fields of endeavor. Many of us became familiar with it as it was popularized by Stephen Covey in his *Seven Habits of Highly Effective People*. Merriam-Webster defines it this way: an important change that happens when the usual way of thinking about or doing something is replaced by a new and different way.

Jesus' main message was the in-breaking of the Kingdom of God, and as he used that term, he introduced and called for a dramatic paradigm shift. Mark's Gospel tells us, "After John was put in prison, Jesus went into Galilee, proclaiming the good news of God. 'The time has come,' he said. 'The kingdom of God has come near. Repent and believe the good news!'" (Mark 1:14–15). What Jesus was bringing was a new and different way. One could only embrace it and enjoy it if he or she was willing to make a drastic change and look at life in a fresh way.

That is what repentance is all about.

Ed Anton described it well as "a cosmic shift of mind and heart."[11] John D. Roth is on the same page when he states: "It [repentance] begins with a recognition that our natural ways of making sense of the world are deeply skewed, and it causes us to reorient our entire perspective in the new light of Christ's living, transforming presence in the world."[12] Later in his book, Roth adds this crucial observation: "Christians in North America have tended to look on faith as something that can improve their lives, not something that might radically reshape their entire worldview.... Only rarely do we consider that the decision to follow Jesus will challenge the very core of our allegiances."[13]

With this in mind, we come to a particularly critical point in Jesus' ministry when he says this to Peter, one of his closest disciples: "Get behind me, Satan! You are a hindrance to me. For you are not setting your mind on the things of God, but on the things of man" (Matthew 16:23 ESV). We will come back to this surprising—even shocking—text later, but what is clear is that Jesus saw that there were two different ways of thinking. The kingdom path is God's way and goes in the opposite direction of man's typical way of thinking. Man's "wisdom" is so opposed to God's that in this instance, it was deserving of the "Satan" label. To follow Jesus is to stop trusting in man's thinking and to give ourselves fully to God's thinking, which means trusting his love and wisdom.

On one occasion, described in John's Gospel, a great number of "disciples" turned back and no longer followed Jesus (6:66). What caused this mass defection? Apparently, the fact that they decided his message was "a hard teaching," asking, "Who can accept it?" (6:60). Like those disciples, we are not going to find God's will as revealed in Jesus' kingdom teaching unless we accept two facts:

1. God's ideas, plans, and wisdom are going to be different from man's.

2. Jesus' teaching will often sound like "hard teaching" to our natural mind.

Our paradigm shift must be so great that we are now putting ourselves completely under God's reign and rule. This will mean we have decided to no longer trust man's logical, rational, and practical wisdom when God through Jesus says something that goes in the opposite direction. We have decided to trust that his wisdom is far higher than man's wisdom no matter how "hard," illogical, or unnatural it may sound to us.

And that leads us to Paul's writings.

Paul to the Corinthians

If there was a center for human wisdom in the ancient Western world, it had to be Greece and specifically, the city of Athens. There in that spot was found the birthplace and home of Western philosophy with its great emphasis on human reason. To their credit, the philosophers no longer wanted to accept the old mythologies but wanted to use reason and logic to analyze the world and search for truth. They had a remarkable impact. The downside of their approach is that it was all about man and his reason, which meant that something we would call "pride" was always at work coloring their efforts. When they took their slant to mathematics, cosmology, and other scientific fields, the results were often good, but when applied to fields like ethics, spirituality, and other metaphysical topics, the effects were more uneven, and certainly far more speculative.

Why is this important to us? First, because our world is still being greatly influenced by that human-centered approach and it is all around us, but, second, because we are about to look at 1 Corinthians, a letter written to disciples in Greece, living just about seventy miles (112 km) from Athens. It is true that Corinth did not have the reputation for intellectual gravitas (or, maybe even, snobbery) like Athens, but we can be sure Corinthian thinking had been influenced by the wisdom emanating from the home of the philosophers.

With that background, it is very instructive that no church we know about in the first century seemed to have more chaos than the one in Corinth. It seems that it was most difficult for the principles of the Kingdom of God to take root in the ground so often sown by the focus on the power of man's reason. So, when the Apostle Paul got word of the disunity, strife, and confusion in this church that he had planted, he wrote with great distress. He first refers to the division among them, then goes straight after their reliance on human wisdom.

> For the message of the cross is foolishness to those who are perishing, but to us who are being saved it is the power of God. For it is written:
>
> > "I will destroy the wisdom of the wise;
> > the intelligence of the intelligent I will frustrate."
>
> Where is the wise person? Where is the teacher of the law? Where is the philosopher of this age? Has not God made foolish the wisdom of the world? For since in the wisdom of God the world through its wisdom did not know him, God was pleased through the foolishness of what was preached to save those who believe. (1 Corinthians 1:18–21)

It seems that the Corinthian confidence in human reason and logic had caused them to reduce their emphasis on the central distinctiveness of the Christian message: *the cross of Christ.* Certainly, nothing would have seemed more irrational and unreasonable than this message that life comes through a cross—a vile example and symbol of Roman power and cruelty, a form of execution that was particularly known as the death of slaves and traitors.

The Corinthian Christians had accepted the message of Jesus, as Paul and his companions had preached it to them, but now societal pressure may have caused them to want their new faith to sound more "reasonable" and sophisticated. Over time (and not that long a time) it appears they pushed the cross to the outer edges. In doing that, they would have not only had a diminished view of Jesus' cross but a failure to understand how important it was for every disciple to go to their own cross and die daily. Thus, with most disciples in the church no longer "taking up the cross" to die to themselves, pride and selfishness had run amok in the church leading to chaos. Without the cross, what was missing was love, that distinctive mark of disciples (John 13:34–35). This prompts Paul's description of true *agape* to burst forth in chapter 13 ("Love is patient, love is kind, it does not envy…") and subsequently roll down through the ages like an ever-flowing stream (with apologies to Amos). When we move away from the "foolishness" of the cross, we move away from radical love.

Nothing Arbitrary

I think it is important to say just here, that there is nothing arbitrary about the cross being at the center of God's wisdom. It is not as though God said, "I'm going to pick the most disgusting and illogical thing I can find and see if people will trust me even in that." No, the cross was the perfect demonstration of God's wisdom because it exemplified self-giving, sacrificial love on the part of the divine. It showed just how far God would go for those who had ignored him or just plain treated him badly. It showed how fully Jesus embraced the wisdom of God, but then as disciples, how fully we must embrace that wisdom. As Paul wrote to the Philippians:

> You should have the same attitude toward one another that Christ Jesus had,
>
>> who though he existed in the form of God
>> did not regard equality with God
>> as something to be grasped,
>> but emptied himself
>> by taking on the form of a slave,
>> by looking like other men,
>> and by sharing in human nature.
>> He humbled himself,
>> by becoming obedient to the point of death
>> —even death on a cross! (Philippians 2:5–8, NET BIBLE)

Rare will be the times when any disciple of Jesus will need to go to a literal cross like he did, but this "attitude…that Christ Jesus had," this refusal to grasp, this willingness to empty himself, this readiness to humble himself, this servant heart, is at the core of the wisdom of God.

Surely, it looked foolish to the human observers for Jesus not to grasp all his divine prerogatives and to hold on to all his rights, but in the wisdom of God there is a much different way to look at the moral universe, and beyond that, the economy of the Kingdom.

> "Whoever finds their life will lose it, and whoever loses their life for my sake will find it."

> "For those who exalt themselves will be humbled, and those who humble themselves will be exalted."

"Unless a kernel of wheat falls to the ground and dies, it remains only a single seed. But if it dies, it produces many seeds."

I feel I must include here John Howard Yoder's statement that we earlier quoted in Volume One:

> Here at the cross is the man who loves his enemies, the man whose righteousness is greater than that of the Pharisees, who being rich became poor, who gives his robe to those who took his cloak, who prays for those who despitefully use him. The cross is not a detour or hurdle on the way to the kingdom, nor is it even the way to the kingdom; it is the kingdom come.[14]

What we see at the cross is the Kingdom come! It is the wisdom and power of God. In one sense, what he did there could never be done by anyone else and does not need to be repeated. The writer of Hebrews says: "He sacrificed for their sins once for all when he offered himself" (7:27b). But the attitude that took him there was not a one-off; it is the heart of the Kingdom. This is the wisdom of God and needs to be seen daily in the lives of disciples in all circumstances. When that happens, the Kingdom *keeps* coming. It keeps showing up in new places. It keeps penetrating the darkness in new ways. It keeps reaching into the hearts of more people.

A Stark Contrast

I have not found another place in Scripture that shows more clearly the contrast between the world's "wisdom" and God's wisdom than the passage cited above from 1 Corinthians 1 and another much like it that we will see in 1 Corinthians 3.

- This message of the cross that is the center of God's wisdom is seen as foolishness by those who are perishing (including the philosophers, as we will see shortly).
- Quoting from Isaiah 29, Paul shows that this wisdom of man will be short-lived. It will be destroyed. The wise man, the scholar, and the philosopher will all be humbled.
- For God has made foolish the wisdom of the world.

Could the contrast be any greater? The world in its wisdom thinks God's message of the cross is foolishness, but God will show that the wisdom of the world is the real foolishness. If I think you are a fool, and you think the same of me, what harmony can we have? The Corinthians seem to be trying to come up with some new religious "alloy" by holding on to some of God's view while freely mixing in the human-centered approach, but it's a fool's errand (pun intended). The two approaches cannot be mixed. The two paths are mutually exclusive.

Paul further addresses the need to focus on the cross in 1 Corinthians 2 along with the implications of retreating from it. Then at the end of chapter 3, he returns to this conflict between human-centered wisdom and that which is God-centered.

> Do not deceive yourselves. If any of you think you are wise by the standards of this age, you should become "fools" so that you may become wise. For the wisdom of this world is foolishness in God's sight. As it is written: "He catches the wise in their craftiness"; and again, "The Lord knows that the thoughts of the wise are futile." (1 Corinthians 3:18–20)

Not only do we find here the caution against living by the world's wisdom, but a warning about being self-deceived. Not surprisingly, the wisdom of the world often is quite appealing to us. It says what our natural person wants to hear. We can deceive ourselves into thinking that we are in fact in the path of wisdom, when in reality we are embracing something that is foolish in God's sight. The path to true wisdom is to confess that on our own, we are really in the place of the "fool."

I find a parallel here to Jesus' first kingdom attitude: "Blessed are the poor in spirit, for theirs is the Kingdom…" (Matthew 5:3). Those who find the Kingdom are those who first acknowledge their own spiritual bankruptcy and emptiness, which means they face the greatness of their need. Those who will find God's wisdom will be those who admit that on their own they are empty of wisdom, thus taking a major step away from being self-deceived.

When Peter Rebuked Jesus

Earlier we noted Jesus' interaction with Peter described in Matthew 16. Let's return there now for a closer look at an incident that serves quite well to illustrate Paul's words to the Corinthians. The story starts with Jesus taking his disciples away from their normal place of ministry. It seems to be a retreat for some time of reflection, and there Jesus asks, "Who do people say the Son of Man is?" (v13). After listening to different reports, he comes back with another question: "But what about you? Who do you say I am?" (v15).

Peter steps up, of course, to say, "You are the Messiah [the Christ], the Son of the living God" (v16), to which Jesus replies, "Blessed are you, Simon son of Jonah, for this was not revealed to you by man, but by my Father in heaven" (v17). But our friend Peter is not doing as well as it appears. Jesus goes on to reveal to him and to the others the events that must unfold to fulfill the messianic mission (the very events the Corinthian Christians will later back away from).

In God's wisdom, Jesus must go to Jerusalem, "suffer many things at the hands of the elders, the chief priests and the teachers of the law, and…he must be killed and on the third day be raised to life" (v21). Peter, in his religious but still worldly wisdom, cannot fathom such an outcome. (Did he miss altogether the part about rising on the third day?) It makes no sense at all to him that the Messiah might have to suffer (no less at the hands of the *Jewish* leaders) and be killed. The way the script was written in his mind, this was irrational, unreasonable, and illogical. In other words, way off track.

Had he just confessed that Jesus was the Messiah of God? Yes. But had Jesus then made a statement that could not be allowed to stand? In Peter's mind, yes. So Peter, seemingly unaware that Jesus would only do and say what was in keeping with God's wisdom, did what you have to do in the face of such a wrong idea. He took Jesus "aside."

Try to grasp this. You have just acknowledged that Jesus is the Messiah, Son of God, and Lord. Now you are gently taking him by the elbow to guide him away from the group, where you might… do what? "Rebuke him," correct him, and show him his thinking is wrong. Maybe quietly, maybe in a whispered tone, maybe in a way not to embarrass, but still to rebuke him, and to say, "Never, Lord!… This shall never happen to you!" To say, "This is just not wise, and you must stop thinking this way."

Peter is the supreme reminder that we can be very religious and be using spiritual words and phrases like "Messiah" and "God" or maybe "God's will" or "God's plan," and still be very much locked in the paradigm of the world and its wisdom. We can see ourselves as spiritually minded, yet say the right things in unpressured situations and then turn to the world's wisdom when the pressure is on or when the stakes get higher—when it becomes a matter of living or dying.

We can deceive ourselves with some fine-sounding arguments. Peter had likely never heard of Athens and the philosophies that came from there, but he was very much living out his street-sense of what the world in its wisdom teaches. It is all about self-reliance, self-preservation, self-defense, self-advancement, self-determination, self-interest, and self-actualization (though Maslow would come much later). The message of self-sacrifice seemed to be for chumps and suckers.

It is at this point that we find Jesus turning to Peter and uttering those words that must have left the apostle stunned: "Get behind me, Satan! You are a stumbling block to me; you do not have in mind the concerns of God, but merely human concerns" (v23). Was Jesus too tough on him? We have to say no, unless we who are disciples want to fall into the same trap Peter did. Understanding the difference between God's way and man's way is so vital that the lines must be drawn clearly. God's wisdom looks foolish if you are looking through human-centered lenses, but when looking through those lenses and acting accordingly, we are line with the evil one, and we must call a spade a spade. "Get behind me, Satan!" Those were the right words.

The Jewish people had been thinking about the coming of the Messiah and the Kingdom of God for hundreds of years. Jesus' "I-must-suffer-and-die" approach was never part of that thinking. Peter was in lockstep with all his Jewish countrymen in his thinking that this was folly. But let us stop and think about it. People like you and me are still talking about and following Jesus all these centuries later. Why? Because Jesus did not trip over Peter's stumbling block but stayed faithful to God's "foolishness."

When we face various questions about kingdom living, we must keep these truths in mind and hold tightly to them. Everywhere we turn we will be faced with powerful temptations to create our own "alloy" that enables us to take hold of Jesus with one hand and take hold of the world's wisdom with the other. This is an extremely easy thing to do. But it is the seriously wrong thing to do.

To overcome our natural tendencies, we must (1) recognize how vulnerable we are to the wrong messages, (2) be a part of a God-focused community and be in close relationships where God's wisdom is constantly reinforced, (3) commit ourselves to being trained in righteousness, and (4) learn to rely on God and the power of the Holy Spirit. To live by the wisdom of the Kingdom does not just happen. However, when these things are true, we can go against the flow and cut against the grain. It will take the full engagement of our soul, mind and heart, but that is what following Jesus and living the kingdom life is all about.

We will need to examine the issues very carefully and prayerfully, not forgetting that God's wisdom will very often seem like foolishness to many. We must remember Paul's caution: "Don't deceive yourselves." We must know that the "foolish" message of the cross is, to us who are being saved, the wisdom and power of God.

This attitude, this wisdom of God, must infuse all our decisions and actions, including those in these circumstances:

- How we react to an offensive comment.
- How we seek to resolve a conflict.
- How we handle business deals.
- How we provide leadership.

- How we handle our family relationships.
- And, not least, how we treat an enemy and how we think about war and violent responses.

Wherever we land regarding military training and service, it must not be because we have had close family members in military service. It must not be because the military gets 85% approval ratings in national polls. It must not be because of some argument for what is pragmatic or because the military makes us feel safer. It must not even be because we know some wonderful disciples who are in the military. We must not make any decision based on the world's wisdom, because to "seek first the Kingdom" means we must be committed to the wisdom of God even when to some it is "foolishness" and "weakness."

3

THE PRINCE OF PEACE
HE IS COMING

Twenty-five-year-old Simon bar Asher farmed with his father on their little patch of land near Capernaum, a city located on the Sea of Galilee. As we count time today, the year was AD 29. Like other Jewish boys in the first century AD, Simon, the son of Asher, grew up hearing that one day God was going to send a messiah, a man especially anointed by God to deliver his people from the obnoxious subordination Israel had been under for so long. This messiah might even be one who would usher in the glorious "age to come," an eternal age of Jewish dominance.

Some of what we are saying here is fact and some is speculation based on facts we have from Scripture and from history. Hopefully, thinking imaginatively about a specific individual like Simon will help us understand Jesus and his times, as well as the Kingdom he preached and lived out. That is because this man we will look at closely eventually became a follower of Jesus, and as a result was transformed to think in completely different ways about the matter of war and violence.

Simon was impulsive, confrontational, and stubborn. He was just the kind of person itching to join a messianic movement. On his heroes list were Joshua and David, but that list also included more recent figures like Judas the Maccabee. All of these were men who led successful military campaigns against the enemies of God's people.

They were men who trained for and waged war. Simon was ready to become one of them.

We began in Chapter 1 noting the appreciation most countries have for their military. Israel in Jesus' day longed to just have a military they could appreciate and be proud of. For 500 years the Jews had been under the thumb of occupiers like the Assyrians, Persians, Ptolemies, and Seleucids. But then Judas "the Maccabee" ("the hammer") and his brothers came on the scene as guerilla-style warriors and led the Jews to nearly fifty years of nation status and independence.

However, by the time of Simon all that had been reversed and now it was Rome that dominated the world—including the Palestine area. When in the cities, Simon saw the Roman soldiers, who reminded him of how brief that freedom had been. His hatred for the Romans was deep. In about 4 BC Rome sent two legions of soldiers from Syria to put down a Jewish revolt in Galilee. Led by the Roman general Publius Quinctilius Varus, the revolt was brutally crushed and ended with the crucifixion of 2,000 Jews. You read that right. Since crucifixions normally took place along roadsides to serve as the maximum warning and deterrent, one can imagine the horror of the scene. This took place before Simon was born, but he grew up hearing much about it. You see, his uncle, his father's brother, Yosef, was one of those crucified and left hanging there to rot. The Romans were easy to hate.

In his teens, Simon hung out with others who were ready to imitate the tactics and valor of men like the Maccabees. Eventually, Simon bar Asher would be known as Simon the Zealot. In the end, he would be part of a great revolution, though not the one he expected.

Before he met Jesus of Nazareth, Simon was no doubt convinced that to be truly free, the Jews needed military power and skill to oust their occupiers and oppressors, and then needed the same thing to maintain their freedom and live as God's people. Independence and liberty could only come through the power of the sword. Among his friends was one Simon bar Jonah, the fisherman, who had grown to have the same conviction. But were they following man's wisdom or God's wisdom?

The Hebrew Scriptures had long predicted, and Simon with other Jewish people had ignored, the coming of a different kind of man and a different kind of kingdom. Aside from Psalms and Deuteronomy, Isaiah is the Old Testament work Jesus quoted most often, and it is Isaiah who gives us the clearest look at the different plan that was in the mind of God.

In Isaiah 2 the prophet envisions a new day, a new community, a new kingdom, and a new attitude. Emphasis has been added in the following quote:

> This is what Isaiah son of Amoz saw concerning Judah and Jerusalem:
>
> In the last days
> *the mountain of the LORD's temple* will be established
>   as the highest of the mountains;
> it will be exalted above the hills,
>   and *all nations* will stream to it.
>
> *Many peoples will come* and say,
>
> "Come, let us go up to the mountain of the LORD,
>   to the temple of the God of Asher.
> He will teach us his ways,

> so that we may walk in his paths."
> The law will go out from Zion,
> > the word of the LORD from Jerusalem.
> He will judge between the nations
> > and will settle disputes for many peoples.
> *They will beat their swords into plowshares*
> > *and their spears into pruning hooks.*
> *Nation will not take up sword against nation,*
> > *nor will they train for war anymore.* (Isaiah 2:1–4)

The mountain here has to be a metaphor for a governing authority (as it is also, even more obviously, in Daniel 2:35), and in this case, it is "the mountain of the Lord," that is, the governing authority of God: his rule, reign, and Kingdom. That it will be "the highest of the mountains" indicates that Mount Zion, the location of Jerusalem, is not literally in mind. At 2510 feet (765 meters), Zion is one of the shorter ones. But this Kingdom that Isaiah can see will be the "highest" and "exalted above the hills" (the lesser kingdoms) because it will be the Kingdom of God with all others subject to it.

Isaiah gives a limited view of the activity there, but it will involve "all nations" and "many peoples." This coming Kingdom will be a gathering of the nations. We should notice the emphasis on the resolution of disputes and the end of hostilities. Whereas the standard understanding of a mighty kingdom would involve the presence of soldiers and armaments to stun its enemies with shock and awe, this kingdom is going to be defined by the transformation of military hardware into agricultural implements—"swords into plowshares;" "spears into pruning hooks."

To use the language that we will find later in the New Testament, in this kingdom the people will say, "Though we live in the world, we do not wage war as the world does. The weapons we fight with are not the weapons of the world" (2 Corinthians 10:3–4). The new Kingdom will still be engaged in a mighty struggle, but all thinking about weaponry and tactics will be transformed. In heaven there will be no AK-47s, bayonets, bombs, or bazookas, and in the Kingdom that breaks in, doing God's will "on earth as it is in heaven," they will not be found. The only battles will be spiritual. Eventually, Simon bar Asher would see this, but he did not quickly embrace the idea that for the greatest revolution, he would not need his sword.

Moving on to Isaiah 9, we find the prophet giving us more understanding of what is coming (again emphasis has been added).

> For to us a child is born,
>   to us a son is given,
>   and the government will be on his shoulders.
> And he will be called
>   Wonderful Counselor, Mighty God,
>   Everlasting Father, *Prince of Peace.*
> *Of the greatness of his government and peace*
>   *there will be no end.*
> *He will reign on David's throne*
>   *and over his kingdom,*
> establishing and upholding it
>   with justice and righteousness
>   from that time on and forever.
> The zeal of the LORD Almighty
>   will accomplish this. (Isaiah 9:6–7)

Let's try to hear through the ears of Simon the Zealot. He likely heard that God is going to send a child who will, of course, first have to grow up (and no longer be a child). The government will be on his shoulders, which means he will have to become older and wiser in the ways of the world and understand that no government can stand without military forces. Anything else would be naïve.

Yes, he will be called Wonderful Counselor, but so was Solomon, a man who also knew the value of the military. (He had 4,000 stalls for war horses, 1,400 chariots and 12,000 horsemen; see 1 Kings 4:26; 10:26.)

Yes, he will be called Mighty God, likely *not* because he will be God, but because he will exercise the mighty power of God as shown in such victories as Gideon over the Midianites, David over the Philistines and Moabites, and Uzziah over the Philistines. Yes, he will be called Everlasting Father, likely because he will become the father of the new restored nation. And, yes, he will be called Prince of Peace (*Sar Shalom*), but who is it that can bring peace? Do we not look around us and see the famous "Pax Romana," the Peace of Rome? And do we not see that it requires overwhelming military force and presence to maintain such peace? Peace almost always comes after you fight for it. Surely, Simon was convinced that a man of war could also be a man of peace and that the first must precede the second.

But Simon would eventually consider a different way of reading this text and see that it describes an entirely different kind of leader who rules with a different spirit. He would continue in Isaiah 11 and see that not only is a child given to us, but he will be one who leads with the humble spirit of a child as well (v6b). He will lead with the nurturing qualities of a Wonderful Counselor and Everlasting Father, and at his heart he will be the Prince of Peace—one consumed not with defeating other people, but doing all he can to bring them together. Of course, it may have taken three years with Jesus for Simon bar Asher to see this, as was also true for his friend, Simon bar

Jonah, the man we know as Peter.

We referred to 9:6 above. Let's get the context by looking at vv5–9. Again emphasis is added.

> Righteousness will be his belt
> and faithfulness the sash around his waist.
> *The wolf will live with the lamb,*
> *the leopard will lie down with the goat,*
> *the calf and the lion and the yearling together;*
> *and a little child will lead them.*
> The cow will feed with the bear,
> their young will lie down together,
> and the lion will eat straw like the ox.
> The infant will play near the cobra's den,
> and the young child will *put* its hand into the viper's nest.
> *They will neither harm nor destroy*
> *on all my holy mountain,*
> for the earth will be filled with the knowledge of the LORD
> as the waters cover the sea. (Isaiah 11:5–9)

In v5 we have another clue, and this time one that shows that a different kind of warfare is to be waged by this Prince of Peace. The belt and sash were foundational elements in the ancient warrior's attire, used not for looks, but to securely hold their weapons. For this Coming One his belt and sash around his waist will be righteousness and faithfulness. *He has already changed his sword into a plowshare and his spear into a pruning hook.* In so doing, he is leading the way.

Isaiah not only describes the Coming One, but also the nature of the Kingdom. In Isaiah's vision, the Kingdom is clearly one where the citizens do not go to war but live in peace with those around them. While the earlier imagery of taking their instruments of war and turning them into farm implements is beautiful, the idea of natural enemies sharing the same space is positively otherworldly: the leopard with the goat, the calf with the lion, the cow with the bear, and the wolf with the lamb (vv6–7). All of this points to a peacemaking and reconciliation of unimaginable dimensions.

This reminds us of Paul's words in Ephesians 3:20 when he speaks of "him who is able to do immeasurably more than all we ask or imagine, according to his power that is at work within us." When the entirety of Ephesians 3 is examined it becomes clear that in context Paul is specifically referring to the unification of people one could never imagine sharing the same space in faith and love. Verse 6 is especially clear: "This mystery is that through the gospel the Gentiles are heirs together with Israel, members together of one body, and sharers together in the promise in Christ Jesus." The wolf with the lamb: unimaginable. The Jews together with the Gentiles in one body: unbelievable. But this is the intention and the power of the Prince of Peace.

We see this in verse 9 of Isaiah 11: "They will neither harm nor destroy on all my holy mountain, for the earth will be filled with the knowledge of the Lord as the waters cover the sea." When the knowledge of the Lord is abundant, as abundant as the oceans, all efforts to harm and destroy will come to an end. To harm and destroy is outside the scope and nature of the Kingdom that will be led by the one we will call Wonderful Counselor, Mighty God, Everlasting Father, Prince of Peace.

Before his meeting with Jesus, we must doubt that Simon bar Asher, aka Simon the Zealot, could even imagine the kingdom Isaiah described, and if he did, he could not imagine it ever including Gentiles, especially the hated Romans.

We don't know what drew him to Jesus. We don't know what caused him to stick around. We don't know how slowly or quickly his mind changed. We know that his fellow disciple and "fellow Simon" was still holding to the old script well along in Jesus' ministry (Matthew 16:22; Mark 8:32). We also know that at some point the words of Isaiah 2, 9 and 11 became flesh for Simon and that he became a zealot for peace, not war.

In the following chapter, we will look at the man Isaiah promised and the man Simon ultimately chose to follow.

4

THE PRINCE OF PEACE
HE HAS COME

In the year AD 66, the Jewish people in Palestine were able to mount their own war of independence against the despised Roman occupiers. Led by the Zealots and, more specifically, by an even more radical group called the Scarii, they attacked first in Jerusalem and then captured the famous fortress of Masada about sixty miles (100 km) to the southeast. According to Josephus, who is our primary source of information about the Jewish-Roman war, they were able to massacre over 700 Romans soldiers during the taking of Masada.

That war with the powerful Romans amazingly dragged on, by some calculations, for nearly eight years until AD 74 with two notable events occurring before its conclusion. First, in AD 70, the Jewish temple was destroyed, never to be rebuilt. Today we can visit the one surviving structure of the temple area—the famous Western Wall. Second, in AD 73 came the siege of Masada. Nearly a thousand Sacarii and Zealots had fled there only to be surrounded by the Romans. In the end, in order not to be killed by the Romans or give them any satisfaction, Josephus tells us that 960 Jewish people voluntarily ended their lives by some combination of killing one another and mass suicide.[16] The story told by the museum historians at Masada today is that only one person committed suicide, the last person, who was drawn by lot. All others were killed by their friends to avoid the sin of suicide.

Had he not made the decision to follow Jesus, the man we are calling Simon bar Asher, the man the Gospel of Luke and the Book of Acts call Simon the Zealot, would very possibly have died at Masada in AD 73. While the Zealot movement that led the Jewish war effort did not fully form until some years after Jesus' time, Simon was likely on a track headed in that direction when his life was interrupted by the teacher from Nazareth.

Into this world of power, war and brutality, into this atmosphere where Simon and his fellows looked for a God-anointed leader of warriors, came Jesus of Nazareth. He *was* a man of strength and power, but of an altogether different nature. He was the fulfillment of those more "peaceful" and "non-warlike" texts in Isaiah that Simon and his furious, insurgent fellows would have found little use for. But something eventually caused Simon to join the Jesus movement, where there was a new way of thinking about the Kingdom.

However it may have come about, we do know that this man zealous for war had some kind of encounter with the Prince of Peace that Isaiah had promised. Simon's conversion to Jesus has not received the kind of ink that we find in the conversion of Saul/Paul, but it may have been no less amazing. Some years ago, in *No One Like Him,* my book on Jesus, I described Jim Woodruff's insightful observation that with Jesus we face many "unbelievables," but also many "undeniables." As we keep looking at him, Woodruff argued, the "undeniables" overcome the "unbelievables." I have to wonder if that was not the experience of Simon ben Asher.

Surely, given his political leanings and family history, he was disturbed by much of Jesus' teaching that sounded to him and his friends like it was weak and toothless. For him it had to be unbelievable that God's Messiah would exalt meekness and humility and speak so favorably of Samaritans and Greeks. He most likely shared the concerns and alarm of Peter (the other Simon) when he heard Jesus talking about suffering and dying voluntarily at the hands of the chief priests and teachers of the law (the wrong people for the Messiah to face off against). And, besides, it was not time to talk of peace when the only peace these Romans knew was peace on their terms, enforced by the sword and the cross. In these matters Simon had no quarrel with the world's wisdom.

But then there were the "undeniables"—Jesus' power over nature and illness and demons, his connection with people, his consistent life, his understanding of men's thoughts, his knowledge of Scripture, his authority shown in interaction with the Pharisees and Sadducees. Maybe Simon was one of those who was not truly converted until the resurrection itself (Luke 22:32), but there was certainly enough to keep him hanging in there. Jesus was likely the wildcard he could not box up, but those "undeniables" just would not go away.

Two Words

To get the full impact of Jesus' radical kingdom teaching, we need to focus on two words and how Simon would have heard them.

1. The first is the word "enemy." Simon and his friends would likely have used this word often, and there would have been no doubt in their minds who the enemy was. Like a modern Muslim extremist, they would have been consumed with the enemy and the desire to obstruct him, disrupt him, drive him out, and kill him. His representatives could be seen throughout Galilee and Judea in their distinctive attire—the short-sleeved knee-length woolen tunic, the iconic iron helmet, the strips of metal that served as armor, the belt to which was attached the double-edged sword. They kept the peace, using whatever brutal methods needed. The Romans occupied the land. One might have enemies even among one's own people, but the Romans were the enemy. When Simon heard Jesus talk about how you treat an enemy, there was one main place his mind would go. Unbelievably, Jesus was saying to love the Romans.

2. The second word is "love." We cannot know how often Simon and his group would have used this word or exactly what it would have meant to them, but we are able to make some educated guesses. The Gospels don't record Jesus using the word all that much. I found him urging or commanding love eight times in the Gospels, if you don't count the duplications. In contrast, Paul uses the word in that way more than fifty times in his letters.

The Hebrew Scriptures talked often of treating others with justice, kindness, or compassion, but what Jesus called "the second great commandment" was rescued from relative obscurity in Leviticus 19:18, where it is a summary statement at the end of a list. It reads, "Do not seek revenge or bear a grudge against anyone among your people, but love your neighbor as yourself."

We do know that a lawyer referenced this "love-your-neighbor" commandment in his conversation with Jesus (Luke 10:26–27), though we quickly learn he was more eager to evade this teaching and justify himself (vv28–29). At the very least the story reminds us that Judaism had some emphasis on love for others, at least for one's neighbor. However, among a subgroup of potential insurgents like Simon and friends, love would not have been very high on the priority list.

So, what was Simon the Zealot to think when he heard Jesus proclaim, "You have heard that it was said, 'Love your neighbor and hate your enemy.' But I tell you: Love your enemies and pray for those who persecute you"? He would have immediately heard two words he knew well: hate and enemies, and they fit together like a hand and glove. The wretched Romans were the enemies and he despised them, their presence, their taxes, their gods, their requirements, their brutality, their crosses, and everything about them.

Perhaps Simon didn't know a lot about love and had not put much emphasis on that whole idea, but when he heard the word, he knew enough to know it was quite different from hate. When Matthew and Luke record this statement of Jesus, they use the Greek word *agape* for the word "love." Jesus would have spoken it originally in Aramaic. My research causes me to think that the Aramaic word Jesus used was likely the word *ahau*, which was a love, like *agape,* that was not necessarily returned. Both refer to doing what is good and best for the other person whether it is of any benefit to oneself or not, and whether or not they respond in any positive way.

Simon may not have been well versed in the concept of love and did not sit around the fire talking about it with the guys, but he had to know something radical was being called for. But maybe radical wasn't the right word. Maybe it was astonishing, ridiculous, or foolish. "Do good to the bloodthirsty Romans? Are you kidding me? Treat them well? Have you lost your mind?"

Here is what we do know for sure: Simon the Zealot was one of the Twelve. He went on to be an apostle. He may have struggled like Peter or Thomas, and really all the rest, but we know he was there after the resurrection with those two and the other eight. He was in the faithful group praying in Jerusalem and waiting for the coming of the Spirit (Acts 1:13–14). He was no Judas. He did not get mad and leave. He did not say, "These are hard teachings. I can't do it." Whether quickly or slowly, we know he changed.

The man who believed you had every right to take up arms

against an evil government and kill the blasphemous enemy, and the man who probably believed it was even a sacred responsibility, became a man who was committed to loving the Romans and every other person who sought to harm him or his loved ones. From all indications, he hung onto the name "the Zealot" (or maybe it hung onto him), but he experienced a massive change of allegiance, so that going forward that moniker was both a reminder of how much he had been transformed and a declaration of how zealous he was for the Prince of Peace and the new Kingdom that Jesus was ushering in.

I have no doubt that a big part of Simon's message was: "Let me tell you what I once believed, and let me tell you how Jesus changed my heart completely." I can easily accept that in the years after the resurrection, as the gospel spread, there was no one who taught more powerfully the message that we must learn war no more but must love our enemies and do good to them.

Going Deeper

I find it most interesting that the first command to love in the Gospel of Matthew and the Gospel of Luke is the command to *love our enemies* and that both occur early in these books as Jesus lays out the overview of the kingdom life. Surely, it was no accident or mistake that Jesus' teaching on love began here. Of course, if this is the way we are to love our enemies, it is clear how we should treat our friends, neighbors, family members, and just the person we encounter randomly on any given day. As we go deeper into his teaching, we find Jesus did not speak in vague terms. He gave specific examples to show just what loving them meant. When we combine the love-your-enemy teaching from Matthew 5 and Luke 6, here is what we find:

1. Do good to those who hate you (Luke 6:27).
2. Pray for those who persecute you or mistreat you (Matthew 5:44; Luke 6:28).
3. Bless those who curse you (Luke 6:28).
4. Lend to them (your enemy) without expecting to get anything back (Luke 6:35).
5. Be merciful as your Father in Heaven is merciful (6:36).
6. Forgive them (Luke 6:37).
7. To not love our enemy in these ways is to be just the same as everyone else and to not do the extraordinary things people in the Kingdom are called to do (Matthew 5:46–47).
8. To do these kinds of things for our enemies is to be like our Father in Heaven (Matthew 5:45, 48; Luke 6:35).

How can we look at such a list and such a posture and not realize that the teaching about the Kingdom of God is the most revolutionary the world has ever heard? It calls for a reexamination of one's whole approach to life. By bringing up love for enemy, Jesus is going to extremes, so let's go to an extreme. We are talking about what you are to do for your cruel, unfeeling enemy who at best wants to control you or ruin you and at worst, to torture you or kill you. He is talking about caring for someone who persecutes you and curses you and maybe even spits on you and calls you disgusting names. He is talking about treating them the way you want to be treated. He's saying this is the kingdom way and the kingdom standard, and that this is what we will do if we are seeking first the Kingdom.

It is one thing to try and ignore an enemy. It is one thing to keep your focus and perspective in the presence of an enemy. It is quite another thing to treat a normally disgusting individual with great kindness and personal regard. It is another thing to do something positive and good for this person even if they could care less. And it is another thing to do it all without any pride or self-righteousness. How counterintuitive is this? How impossible does this sound? The call to this kind of approach drives us back to the first beatitude where we confess our poverty of spirit and deep need for God's help (Matthew 5:3). "God have mercy on me. Fill me with your Spirit. I am unable to love like this!" But that brings the kingdom life ("theirs is the Kingdom") and it will be precisely there that we will find the power to do the extraordinary, as the early Christians did.

Justin Martyr, writing about AD 160, shows that God gives the power to be different. He put it this way: "We who formerly murdered one another now refrain from making war even upon our enemies.... We used to be filled with war, mutual slaughter, and every kind of wickedness. However, now all of us have, *throughout the whole earth,* changed our warlike weapons. We have changed our swords into plowshares, and our spears into farming implements" (emphasis added). Just as he says, his sentiments were widely shared in the church in its first three hundred years. They saw that they had to love their enemies, and to paraphrase C.S. Lewis, "If something has to be done, there is no use talking about whether or not it can be done." If they were to love their enemies, they would have to start by not making war on them. It should go without saying that step one is not to kill the person you are called to love. Of course, that is only step one, and the early disciples went much further than that.

As hard as it is to fathom, somewhere along the line, Simon the Zealot could be found praying for his Roman occupiers. He likely prayed that he would be respectful to them and have a positive attitude about carrying their gear the required one mile, and even prayed he would be extraordinary, and would offer to carry it a second mile. He prayed that he would treat them as people with families and needs and emotions. He prayed he would see them as souls, souls that could be redeemed and brought out of darkness into the light. Given the transformations we have seen in our own day, is it so hard to imagine that one of Simon's most consistent prayers would be for Jesus to use him to bring Roman soldiers to the foot of the cross, where this time they would be there for a whole different purpose? Is it so hard to believe that Simon the Zealot helped Romans soldiers to be buried with Christ in baptism and raised to a new life?

Some Zealots were known to carry small swords that could be hidden beneath their robes. It was not uncommon for a Zealot to stand next to a soldier in a crowd and at the right time, slide it out of his robe into the body of the soldier and then flee, not unlike some modern-day terrorists. At some point we can well imagine that Simon gave up his sword. He may have still had it in Luke 22:38 when the disciples said, "See, Lord, here are two swords." One may have been his and the other Peter's (John 18:10). However, after hearing Jesus say, "All who draw the sword will die by the sword" (Matthew 26.52), Simon may have seen no need to keep it. In the new kingdom Isaiah had looked forward to, the very one Jesus was bringing, you would never use it on an enemy, but would treat your enemy like your friend.

New Role

What Simon learned is that when you become a disciple of Jesus your role in the world is radically changed. You are now a disciple of the Prince of Peace and your main role is now to be a peacemaker—one who brings people to peace with God and peace with one another. Paul would later understand this and state it this way:

> So from now on we regard no one from a worldly point of view. Though we once regarded Christ in this way, we do so no longer. Therefore, if anyone is in Christ, the new creation has come: The old has gone, the new is here! All this is from God, who reconciled us to himself through Christ and gave us the ministry of reconciliation: that God was reconciling the world to himself in Christ, not counting people's sins against them. And he has committed to us the message of reconciliation. We are therefore Christ's ambassadors, as though God were making his appeal through us. We implore you on Christ's behalf: Be reconciled to God. (2 Corinthians 5:16–20)

Simon was now an ambassador of the Prince of Peace, as are we, who are also disciples of Jesus. Our Lord is in the business of reconciliation, and now that is also our business and our role. Some things we were doing before our role changed are not inconsistent with that new mission, but some things no longer fit. Simon's role as a would-be political liberator was so at odds with his new role as peacemaker that it had to be given up. Paul's dictum, "Each person should remain in the situation they were in when God called them" (1 Corinthians 7:20), was not an absolute rule. One cannot continue in anything that is at odds with the new ministry of reconciliation and new role as ambassador of peace.[17]

A Different End

If Simon had stayed on the Zealot track, he might very well have died on the high and spectacular plateau of Masada…*for a lost cause.* As it is, we know he became a disciple and apostle of Jesus. He came to know the Prince of Peace, and he went forth preaching the gospel of the Kingdom and the gospel of peace.

The most widespread tradition says Simon was martyred in Egypt along with the Apostle Jude in AD 65. No matter the way he died and wherever it may have been, it was for a cause that endures to this day and is still calling men and women everywhere to be reconciled to God, to put down their weapons, to love their enemies, and to learn war no more.

5

THE TEACHING OF THE EARLY CHURCH

As we pursue kingdom living and obedience to Jesus, our ultimate authority is found in his words and the words of Scripture. There is also value in seeing how believers through history processed those words. So, we ask, what do we find about Christians and the military in the times closest to Jesus' life—the second and third centuries? Do we find that those Christians in the first two or three centuries really embraced the principle of peace or did they soon depart from this most "impractical" way of living? Was it found to be an impossible ethic?

Fortunately, we have the works of those we often call the church fathers. These leaders left us with writings and teachings on a variety of subjects including the one we are addressing in this book. The Roman Empire had a powerful world presence, and a robust military was a key to their success. The early church grew and spread in this environment. The invasion of the Kingdom of God clashed with the power of Rome on many points, and the works of the church fathers illustrate that kingdom ideas about enemies and the military were in sharp contrast with those of the empire.

Let me be open here. One of my early readers let me know that he did not find this chapter to be persuasive, and dismissed it from the get-go. He is a fair-minded person, so hear his reasoning. He argues that we aren't dealing with Scripture at this point and that by careful selection you can use early church writings to buttress many conflicting viewpoints. For him, I was better off deleting this chapter. Was he right? Does it matter what the early church believed? We can agree that these believers were not writing Scripture. We are not basing our lives and the practice of our churches on Justin, Clement, Tertullian, or Origen. They believed and taught some things that I do not believe and will not teach today. So, why does it matter what they taught and did regarding soldiering and war?

Let us say clearly that it is not enough for us to be Christian pacifists because that is what the church of the first three centuries taught and practiced. We should only take that position if it fits with the message of Jesus and is a part of living out his Kingdom in the here and now. However, I find it significant that in a violent world where they were often the object of the violence, Christians of the first three hundred years held on to this nonviolent message and only gave it up when their faith and the politics of this world, with its "wisdom," were mixed together beginning with the Emperor Constantine, who brought church and empire together in an unholy alliance.

In some cases, it appears the early church made decisions for worldly reasons. In the case of the church holding to nonviolence, it seems clear that they made *this* decision purely because they were seeking to be faithful to Jesus as Lord and to do God's will on earth as it is in heaven. There was no earthly reason and no argument from philosophy that would have led them to this commitment. It appeared weak, foolish, and irrational. It was ridiculed. But when the world's wisdom and God's wisdom clashed, they held on to the "foolishness" of God's wisdom—at least in this case.

Quite often the early church writers put the emphasis on Jesus' words of peace, non-resistance, and enemy-love from the Sermon on the Mount. At other times they quote from Isaiah (or Micah) about swords being transformed into plowshares to show that the kingdom life is oriented toward peace.

One of the earliest extrabiblical Christian works is from the late part of the first century and is known as the *Didache,* or by its other title, *The Teachings of the Twelve Apostles.* We don't know its author (or authors) but scholars date it between AD 80 and 90. The opening words of this echo the words of Jesus in Matthew's gospel, and we can see that the church was putting front and center Jesus' challenging teaching about how to treat an enemy.

> This is the way of life: first, you shall love the God who made you, secondly, your neighbor as yourself: and all things whatsoever you would not should happen to you, do not thou to another. The teaching of these words is this: Bless those who curse you, and pray for your enemies, and fast on behalf of those who persecute you: for what thanks will be due to you, if you love only those who love you? Do not the Gentiles also do the same? But love those who hate you, and you shall not have an enemy.[18]

Clement of Alexandria, writing about AD 195, said, "He bids us to 'love our enemies, bless those who curse us, and pray for those who despitefully use us.'" He elaborates on Jesus' words when he writes, "'If anyone strikes you on the one cheek, turn to him the other also, and if anyone takes away your coat, do not hinder him from taking your cloak also.' An enemy must be aided so that he may not continue as an enemy. For by help, good feeling is compacted and enmity dissolved."[19]

Justin Martyr (AD 100–165) was born in Palestine, but died for his faith in Rome. He alludes to Isaiah 2 when he says:

> We ourselves were well conversant with war, murder and everything evil, but all of us throughout the whole wide earth have traded in our weapons of war. We have exchanged our swords for plowshares, our spears for farm tools. Now we cultivate the fear of God, justice, kindness, faith, and the expectation of the future given us through the Crucified One…. The more we are persecuted and martyred, the more do others in ever increasing numbers become believers.[20]

Later he added: "We who formerly treasured money and possessions more than anything else, now hand over everything we have to a treasury for all and share it with everyone who needs it. We who formerly hated and murdered one another now live together and share the same table. We pray for our enemies and try to win those who hate us."[21]

One of the more interesting documents that we have from the late 100s or early 200s is something known as the Apostolic Traditions. Most scholars believe it was written by Hippolytus of Rome (170–236) and it is basically a manual for church life including instructions about worship. It contains this passage that is relevant for us: "The professions and trades of those who are going to be accepted into the community must be examined. The nature and type of each must be established." Then there are listed different professions that must be given up by Christians, including: keeper of a brothel, sculptor of idols, charioteer, athlete, gladiator; and each time it states "give it up or be rejected." Then we have this: "A military constable must be forbidden to kill, neither may he swear; if he is not willing to follow these instructions, he must be rejected. A proconsul or magistrate who wears the purple and governs by the sword shall give it up or be rejected."

And then a bit later he writes: "Anyone taking part in baptismal instruction or already baptized who wants to become a soldier shall be sent away, for he has despised God." Another version of this document adds this: "A soldier in the sovereign's army should not kill or if he is ordered to kill, he should refuse. If he stops, so be it; otherwise, he should be excluded." Other practices are then listed as unacceptable: prostitute, sodomite, magician, and soothsayer. All these must be given up.[22]

Preston Sprinkle argues that the Apostolic Traditions is important because it shows us what was going on down at the local church level and not just what was being taught by the church theologians.[23]

Cyprian (200–258), who was the bishop of Carthage in North Africa, compared killing in war with murder with this pointed comment:

> We are scattered over the whole earth with the bloody horror of camps. The whole world is wet with mutual blood. And murder—which is admitted to be a crime in the case of an individual—is called a virtue when it is committed wholesale. Impunity is claimed for wicked deeds, not because they are guiltless—but because the cruelty is perpetrated on a grand scale![24]

For Cyprian, as for most early church writers and leaders, the problem was killing, and he found it odd that killing an individual in daily life is universally rejected while the wholesale killing that goes on in war is exalted.

In another place he addressed the enemies of the faith: "None of us offers resistance when he is seized, or avenges himself for your unjust violence, although our people are numerous and plentiful.... It is not lawful for us to hate, and so we please God more when we render no requital for injury.... We repay your hatred with kindness."[25] In this, he found the uniqueness of Jesus' ethic.

Tertullian (160–220) was raised by pagan parents, and he did not become a Christian until sometime in his late thirties or early forties. Nevertheless, he became one of the most prolific writers in the early church. He is sometimes called the Father of Western Theology and the Father of Latin Christianity. He was the first of these leaders to write most of his works in Latin. He eventually left the mainstream church and became part of the Montanist movement because he felt the majority was turning in a worldly direction.

Particularly after he joined the Montanists, he wrote much about the need for Christians to avoid war. He wrote an entire treatise titled *The Crown,* in which he spelled out the Christian case against military involvement. Here is a sampling of the points that he made in that work and in other writings:

- "If then, we are commanded to love our enemies, whom have we to hate? If injured, we are forbidden to retaliate, lest we become just as bad ourselves. Who can suffer injury at our hands."[26]

- "Only without the sword can the Christian wage war: the Lord has abolished the sword. Christ, in disarming Peter, disarmed every soldier."[27]

- "But now inquiry is being made concerning these issues. First, can any believer enlist in the military? Second, can any soldier, even those of the rank and file or lesser grades who neither engage in pagan sacrifices nor capital punishment, be admitted into the church? No on both counts—for there is no agreement between the divine sacrament and the human sacrament, the standard of Christ and the standard of the devil, the camp of light and the camp of darkness. One soul cannot serve two masters—God and Caesar.... But how will a Christian engage in war (indeed, how will a Christian even engage in military service during peacetime) without the sword, which the Lord has taken away?"[28]

- "Shall it be held lawful to make an occupation of the sword, when the Lord proclaims that he who uses the sword shall perish by the sword? And shall the son of peace take part in the battle when it does not become him even to sue at law?"[29]

- "Will those who are forbidden to engage in a lawsuit espouse the deeds of war? Will a Christian who is told to turn the other cheek when struck unjustly, guard prisoners in chains, and administer torture and capital punishment?"[30]

Tertullian's arguments revolved around three points: (1) Jesus' command for us to love enemies, (2) Jesus' call for Peter to put down the sword while condemning those who lived by the sword, and (3) Jesus' overall ethic involving non-resistance and non-retaliation.

Sometimes it is said that Tertullian and other writers were mainly concerned about the idolatry that was a consistent part of Roman military experience—something that would not be found in the military today. There is no doubt that this was a concern, and Tertullian addresses that in *The Crown* and in *On Idolatry,* but from the quotes we have here, we can see that his objections to the military were not limited to that concern.

Some who don't believe Tertullian to be useful in this discussion often point out that he also forbids a Christian to be a schoolmaster, a teacher of literature, or a seller of frankincense, and that he condemns all forms of painting, modeling, and sculpture. The argument is if he was wrong about these, then he was also wrong about the military. However, one must consider how biblically based was his critique of military service, while his condemnation of other things was more based on his general concern for how far the church was drifting in worldly directions.

Origen (185–254) was even more prolific than Tertullian, writing an astonishing 2,000-plus treatises on nearly every biblical subject imaginable. His works contain a great many comments related to our topic. Here are some of those:

- "Yet Christ nowhere teaches that it is right for his disciples to offer violence to anyone, no matter how wicked. For he did not consider it to be in accord with his laws. To allow for the killing of any individual whomever for his laws are derived from a Divine source… For his laws do not allow them on any occasion to resist their persecutors even when it is their fate to be slain as sheep."[31]

- "To those who ask us whence we have come or whom we have for a leader, we say that we have come in accordance with the counsels of Jesus to cut down our warlike and arrogant swords of argument into ploughshares, and we convert into sickles the spears we formerly used in fighting. For we no longer take 'sword against a nation,' nor do we learn 'any more to make war,' having become sons of peace for the sake of Jesus, who is our leader, instead of following the ancestral customs in which we were strangers to the covenants."[32]

- "To this our answer is, we do give help to Kings when needed. But this is so to speak, a Divine help, 'putting on the whole armor of God.'" Origin then mentions Paul's command for us to pray for those in authority and ends with this statement: "This is a greater help than what is done by soldiers who go forth to kill as many of the enemy as they can."[33]

- "How was it possible for the gospel doctrine of peace to prevail throughout the world? For it does not permit men to take vengeance even on their enemies."[34]

The man who has been described as "the greatest genius the early church ever produced" consistently opposed Christian participation in military activities. He was tortured for his faith during the Decian persecution in 250 and died three to four years later from his injuries.

Lactantius (c.250–c.325) is our main example of a church father whose early writing occurred before Constantine and his later work after the edict of Constantine in the new era when the Christian Church was viewed favorably by the empire. In his *Divine Institutes*, written in the earlier period, he makes as strong a statement as we can find, writing,

> It is not right for a just man to serve in the army.... Nor is it right for a just man to charge someone with a capital crime. It does not matter whether you kill a man with the sword or with a word, since it is killing itself that is prohibited. So

there must be no exception to this command of God. Killing a human being whom God willed to be inviolable [some translations: "a sacred animal"] is always wrong.[35]

After Constantine experienced his "conversion" and gave the edict legalizing Christianity, he asked Lactantius to become his spiritual advisor, tutor his son, and help shape the church's relationship to the empire. At some point we find Lactantius changing his posture. In his Epitome, he writes: "Just as courage is good if you are fighting for your country but evil if you are rebelling against it, so too with the emotions. If you use them for good ends, they will be virtues; if for evil ends, they will be called vices."[36] In other places we see that he no longer opposed all violence. Pacifists see this as an example of letting politics take priority over conviction. They see how gaining power has a corrupting effect, and here is an example of what happened to the church in general in the era of Constantine. Others argue he was just faithfully adapting to new circumstances.

So, what is our conclusion? First, there is a united message from the church fathers of the first three centuries that the disciple of Jesus does not kill his enemy, but loves him. Let's hear from Roland Bainton, the renowned church historian. In his *Christian Attitudes toward War and Peace,* he has a chapter titled "The Pacifism of the Early Church," where he makes the following assertion:

> The three Christian positions with regard to war…matured in chronological sequence, moving from pacifism to the just war to the Crusade. The age of persecution down to the time of Constantine was the age of pacifism to the degree that during this period no Christian author to our knowledge approved of Christian participation in battle.[37]

From my study it seems that the first notable Christian writer who explicitly gives approval to Christian soldiering and killing is Athanasius (296–373), who is often called the Father of Orthodoxy. All his writings took place well into the Constantinian era, with his first treatise being written in 319. In his *Letter 48* he states:

> It is not right to kill, yet in war it is lawful and praiseworthy to destroy the enemy; accordingly, not only are they who have distinguished themselves in the field held worthy of great honors, but monuments are put up proclaiming their achievements. So that the same act is at one time and under some circumstances unlawful, while under others, and at the right time, it is lawful and permissible.

While in the Constantinian era most church leaders came to support this view of Athanasius, there were some who continued to oppose military service. But gradually, there were fewer and fewer who agreed with the pacifist position.

After Jesus, we have the *Didache,* Justin Martyr, and Clement of Alexander saying, follow Jesus and "love your enemies and pray for them." Then later—but not until well into the fourth century—we have a leader of the church saying it is praiseworthy to destroy the enemy. The United States of America has been a country for two hundred and forty-three years. To those of us who live here, we sense that this a long time. Yet for almost *three hundred years* Christians taught that they were to love their enemies and not kill them. But then came a great shift—what scholars call the Constantinian Shift. The emperor befriended the church, and most church leaders embraced the empire, including its war machine.

Second, we need to be transparent about the fact that there were

Christians who were in the Roman army during the first three centuries. A story, describing events from about 173, appears in Cassius Dio's *Roman History* describing the seemingly miraculous rescue of a Roman legion. As the story spread, credit was given, at least by some, to the prayers of Christian soldiers. This is the story of the so-called "Thundering Legion," whose enemy was supposedly driven away by the sudden appearance of a violent thunderstorm.

Tertullian wrote his *The Crown* because of a story he had heard about a soldier who was a Christian and was eventually put to death. Tertullian indicates this soldier was not the only Christian in that force. There are a number of indications that Christians joined the army between 175 and 313, but there are many who say that this was part of a broader moral laxness that began to permeate the church. The persecution of Christians under Diocletian (who became emperor in 284 and initiated the persecution in 303) is known to have begun in the army. Before he moved on to the general population, he wanted to be sure that all Christians had been purged from the military, clear evidence of the presence of believers in the army of the empire.

However, the presence of confessing Christians in the army is no more an argument against the pacifism of the early church than the presence of sexual immorality in the church in Corinth is an argument against the first-century church's teaching on sexual purity. Just because certain individuals did not live out the message that was taught does not nullify the fact that the message was taught. The church regularly fails to live up to its teaching. I have to admit that I am perplexed when people supportive of the pro-military position seem eager to discount the value of the early church writers, yet want to emphasize that there were Christians in the army in the second and third centuries. Seems to me that you can't have it both ways.

Third, we can conclude that while Christian practice was not always consistent, the normal posture in the early church was one of pacifism until the time of Constantine. We see that there was a unified message from the leading teachers in the church. *We have no writer or leader in almost three hundred years who approved of violence.* Even the early church's critics show us the believers took a pacifist position. Celsus, a Greek philosopher writing about 178, attacked the church for its practice of not serving in the army, arguing that if all people did as the Christians, the emperor would be deserted, and his realm would fall prey to savages and barbarians. (By the way, that is still an argument used against Christian pacifists today.) We know as much about Celsus as we do because later Origen would respond to his various attacks, including this one. Some of the quotes from Origen mentioned earlier were in reply to this very point. While there were exceptions, the Christian movement was known for its commitment to peace, non-resistance, and nonviolence, and that stance greatly troubled an opponent like Celsus.

While the early church leaders were united in their message of enemy-love and nonviolence, the Christian world has been equally united for the last seventeen hundred years in defending Christians who train for and go to war. Only here and there have small minorities resisted this idea, and they have often been regarded as rather odd. It should, however, be said that in recent decades, there has been a resurgence of support for the pacifist view outside the so-called "peace churches." For our purposes, it is important to note that this development has been closely linked to greater emphasis on Jesus' kingdom teaching.

Following Constantine, the idea of "just war" was adopted and has been the flag under which many have gone off to fight for centuries, more often than not against other "Christians." We will examine that theory or teaching in the following chapter.

Before we turn to that historical shift, I would leave us with this question: Do we find anything in the teachings of Jesus and his gospel of the Kingdom that would cause us to move away from the pacifist teaching that we find in the second- and third-century church leaders? At least on this point, were they showing us how to live out the teachings of Jesus in this present age?

6

JUST WAR THEORY

As long as Christian writers supported nonviolence as a basic principle for disciples, there was no need on their part to make any argument for war or to defend the morality of war under certain circumstances. Accordingly, there is no example that I know of in which a Christian writer makes a case for a just war during the almost three-hundred-year period to which we have often referred. *However, once the church became allied with the state, that all changed.* With professing Christians eventually being encouraged to enter the army, there had to be an explanation for why they could take the lives of others. It was here that "just war theory" entered the world of Christian teaching.

What we will look at in this chapter is important because *if you do not accept the nonviolent, pacifist position, your only alternative as a professing follower of Jesus will be to embrace some iteration of just war theory.* The question will be: Is this a good answer for disciples of Jesus? The question will be: Does just war theory allow you to kill in war and still be faithful to God's Kingdom breaking into the world?

Christians did not originate the idea of a "just war." Aristotle (384–322 BC) seems to be the first to use the phrase. His thinking about just war lacks many of the essential elements that would become part of Christian just war theory. For example, he did not object to all wars of aggression. However, as one concerned about morality, Aristotle saw that because of its very nature, war is something that must be justified ethically. In the process of trying to do that, he concluded that some wars are unjust and some are just. Other Greeks and also Romans, including the philosopher and orator Cicero (106–43 BC), continued discussions about what was just and unjust in war.[38]

A heads-up for you: You may not find the following discussion to be the most stimulating, but if you intend to seriously engage the issue before us, you need to understand what we will discuss. Most people assume *their* country fights just wars. You need to examine this. Open a window, let in some cool air, get a cup of coffee or tea, stay awake, and wade in!

Augustine of Hippo

Building on the foundations of Aristotle and Cicero, Augustine (AD 354–430) would become the so-called Father of Christian Just War Theory. While Augustine believed that Jesus taught nonviolence, he came to also believe that Jesus' message was intended for those who lived under non-Christian government, and that it had to be adapted to the new situation when the empire itself was led by believers. As individuals, Christians should continue to practice nonviolence and not engage in self-defense. However, a nation can hardly exist without an army and a willingness to defeat enemies that threaten that nation. By the time of Augustine, the power of Rome was weakened, and the empire was often in danger of attack from other forces. He saw no virtue in allowing their Christian society to be destroyed.

With Christianity now the official religion, a Christian military was needed to repel the invaders. In 416 an edict was issued banning anyone from the army who was a pagan and not a Christian, but things had been moving in that direction for some time. Augustine believed Christians must despise war and want to avoid it. However, in a Christian nation or commonwealth, he reasoned that there must be a just way that they can fight and kill their enemies and protect their people. In other words, there are certain Christian principles to be kept even in an activity that is repugnant to a Christian.

His thoughts about this are found primarily in his most famous work, *The City of God*. A word of caution is in order: Don't be misled by certain internet articles. Augustine never gave a full definition of a just war. That would not come for several centuries with the work of Thomas Aquinas, but many people who write on just war today, particularly on the internet, blend the work of the two theologians together. However, Augustine does give various principles, although not systematically, that he believes must be involved.

He speaks out against destroying and looting conquered cities. He also forbids robbing, killing, and raping those who are defeated. All of these were quite acceptable in his world, but he called on Christians to exhibit mercy and restraint. For Augustine, peace must be a major goal of war. The end that is sought must be peace, not domination (and certainly not enslavement). The following quote is often used to summarize his viewpoint: "We do not seek peace in order to be at war, but we go to war that we may have peace. Be peaceful, therefore, in warring, so that you may vanquish those whom you war against, and bring them to the prosperity of peace." The goal of war must be to restore the natural order, and the natural order is a condition of peace.

In *Letter 138* to Marcellinus, Augustine writes, "If the earthly city [the Christian state] observes Christian principles, even its wars will be waged with the benevolent purpose that better provision might be made for the defeated to live harmoniously together in justice and godliness."[39] This emphasis on peace seems quite reassuring, but is not so much that way when we realize that *Letter 138* was written to assure Marcellinus that using violence against heretics is consistent with Christianity and is for their own good. In this case the violence was to be used against the Donatists, a "rigorous" Christian group that believed the church had become lax and tolerant of sin and had separated itself from the church hierarchy.

If that is not remarkable enough, there is something else quite surprising, considering the high place Augustine is given in church history: for Augustine, a war could be seen as just if it brought about a peace that enabled Christian authorities *to compel* people to become Christians, since that was for their good and the good of society. In this, he seems to be borrowing from Cicero, who believed it was right to compel people to be more virtuous. Astonishingly, Augustine would go on to advocate fines, imprisonment, banishment, and "moderate" floggings to be used if they would bring about conversions. Also, from *Letter 138*, we find him writing, "We often have to act with a sort of *kindly harshness,* when we are trying to make *unwilling souls yield,* because we have to consider their welfare rather than their inclination" (emphasis added). Sadly, the man who preached salting war with peace and mercy would pave the way for many unfortunate stories of forced conversions during the centuries that followed. But this does show us that for Augustine a war was just if it both caused people to come to God (even if by force) and restored the moral order.

We should add that for Augustine war initiated to punish a people for their evil deeds was also to be considered a just war. As one can imagine, this opens the door to a great deal of subjectivity and disagreements. You are left with a situation where one state judges the guilt of another. Naturally a state always sees itself as the innocent one and the enemy as the guilty one, so this argument virtually gives any state *carte blanche* to start a war. In spite of the weakness of this idea, Aquinas, and later even the reformers Luther and Calvin, would support it.

Throughout Augustine's works he repeatedly emphasizes that the real problem with war is not the outward destruction that it brings but the inward damage it does to the heart and soul. A just war is waged only by those who keep the heart free from hate, revenge, and other evils. Outwardly, one might be doing great damage, but if within they were keeping their heart in line with the Spirit, their deeds did not matter that much. However, such emphasis on what goes on within did not and does not lead to any guidelines that can collectively be useful, and certainly has the taste of Gnostic dualism. Luther will later make a similar argument that continues to be popular today: one's outward actions are one thing; what kind of heart one has is another.

Before we leave Augustine, we should add that he places the responsibility for a just war on the authorities at the top and removes it from the individual soldier. The authorities (king, emperor, etc.) should decide if a matter is divinely sanctioned and if the action is just. Once that decision is made, it is the soldier's job to obey orders. He assumes that the governing authorities will have concern for doing the will of God.

How should we think of Augustine and his view of just war? He wasn't the first to say that Christians could and even should fight, but he did say that a certain amount of reflection ought to go on before that. He did say that, in particular, government leaders needed to make some moral decisions based on some general Christian principles before and during war. However, when it came to application, he left a lot of murky ideas that did little to restrain the wars that "Christians" engaged in during the following centuries.

Thomas Aquinas

The Christian thinker who has done the most to shape just war theory as it is found today is Thomas Aquinas, the thirteenth-century Italian theologian. Aquinas addresses the matter of war primarily in his famous and lengthy *Summa Theologica.*

Organizing Augustine's thought, Aquinas said that there are three requisites for a war to be just. All of these fit into the category usually described with the Latin phrase, *jus ad bellum,* which literally means "the right to war."

1. *War must be declared by the proper authority.* Individuals cannot initiate war. War can only be declared, and the people of a commonwealth mustered to fight it, if it comes from the "princes" to whom such responsibility for government has been entrusted.

2. *There must be a just cause for war,* "so that they who are assailed should deserve to be assailed for some fault that they have committed." Aquinas quotes Augustine, who says: "Just wars are usually defined as those which avenge injuries, in cases where a nation or city has to be chastised for having either neglected to punish the wicked doings of its people, or neglected to restore what has been wrongfully taken away." So we see that Aquinas agrees with Augustine that a war can be just if it is to punish wrong or to reclaim stolen property. It is interesting that he seems to assume, since he does not mention it, that self-defense is proper enough reason to go to war. If you can start a war for these other reasons, surely you can justly engage in war if someone else attacks you. Modern formulations often state that "the damage inflicted

by the aggressor on the nation or community of nations must be lasting, grave, and certain" in order to have a just cause.

3. *There must be a right intention of promoting good or avoiding evil.* Again, he quotes Augustine, who says: "Eagerness to hurt, bloodthirsty desire of revenge, an untamed and unforgiving temper, ferocity in renewing the struggle, dust of empire—these and the like excesses are justly blamed in war." One of his three requirements is an inward attitude of the heart (presumably on the part of the leader who initiates and prosecutes a war) that is not sinful, but is seeking righteousness. Just intention would be demonstrated if the winning side does not go beyond reasonable bounds and does not exceed the just cause for which the war was fought.

To these three requirements, eventually a fourth idea was added by others and that is *for a war to be just, it must be a matter of last resort.* In other words, war should only be started when other, nonviolent methods to resolve a matter have failed. To put it another way, all other means of putting an end to the dispute must have been shown to be impractical or ineffective.

While you do find this last one on most descriptions of just war today, it is not without controversy. Some insist that you must add that war may be started after making a last attempt that "has some reasonable hope of success." Others feel that it is impossible to know when you are at a point of "last resort," so that this requirement may only be delaying action while something evil continues.

Aquinas' three elements plus "the last resort" compose the four factors found in *jus ad bellum* in most just war theories. To summarize, just war can only be initiated when these elements are present:

1. Right authority
2. Just cause
3. Right intention
4. Done as a last resort

Justice in War and After War

A just war, however, according to most proponents of this theory, requires more than merely the right reasons to go to war. *Jus in bello* is justice in war, referring to correct conduct in battle once the decision to go to war has been made, and this must be the concern of combatants, officers as well as soldiers. The idea here is that while a nation may satisfy the requirements of *jus ad bellum,* it still must conduct itself justly in the war to satisfy just war theory. Both Augustine and Aquinas addressed these matters, arguing that it is not true that "all is fair in war." Even in war, there must be limits, and the humanity of the enemy must be respected. Even if you kill, there are certain things you are not free to do.

As it later came to be formulated, *jus in bello* usually includes:

1. *Proportionality:* The degree of allowable force used in the war must be measured against the force required to fulfill the just cause. Here we have somewhat of an application of "an eye for an eye" (*lex talionis*). If the damage done by a belligerent was X then your response should not be X+Y+Z or 4X. If they destroyed a village, you must not destroy a city, unless there is no other way to defeat them. The players in a war must measure and remeasure their actions, with an eye toward keeping their responses proportional to the instigation, always guarding against excessive force.

2. *Discrimination* (sometimes called distinction): Belligerents must always distinguish between military and civilian objectives, and intentionally attack only military objectives.

3. *Responsibility:* A country is not responsible for unexpected side effects of its military activity as long as the following three conditions are met:
   (a) The action must carry the intention to produce good consequences.
   (b) The bad effects were not intended.
   (c) The good of the war must outweigh the damage done by it. The use of arms must not produce evils and disorders graver than the evil to be eliminated.

If you research the just war literature, you will sometimes find other ways of describing the theory and other elements sometimes added, but I have tried to give you the basic approach.

So, beginning with *jus da bellum* and *jus in bello,* we now find that a third category has more recently entered discussion: *Jus post bellum* or justice after war. This is beyond the scope of our inquiry, but it is concerned with making a just peace and the responsibility and accountability of the parties after war has ended.

On the Plus Side of Just War Theory

How should a disciple of Jesus evaluate just war theory? As I said at the beginning of this chapter, if we reject the nonviolent, pacifist approach, the just war argument is our only alternative. There are other theories about the morality of war, like the realist approach or that of what is called "positive law" and the revolutionary theory of war advocated by Lenin, but these are entirely secular and are of no use to a Christian. There is a Chinese, as well as Islamic, tradition of just war, but for obvious reasons a Christian will find little help from them, as well.

Given the overall tone of this book, what I am going to say next may surprise you. The more I have considered just war theory the more I have come to appreciate it. I see it seriously trying to grapple with a serious dilemma—how can it be moral for Christians to kill their enemies? And what may be more surprising is that the most compelling arguments I have heard for just war theory have come from writers taking the pacifist position. So, in evaluating just war theory, I can list several items on the positive side:

1. We can appreciate that just war theory begins with a concern about a moral question. When thinking about participating in some action that will likely bring about many deaths, injuries, and disfigurements, it is crucial to stay focused on moral principles.

2. All just war theory seeks to limit the impact of war. Within the theory is the idea of stopping evil, without giving in to evil and letting it run amok. War stirs evil in the hearts of people like nothing else. Wars notoriously get completely out of control, so we have horrors like the Crusaders' slaughter of 70,000 men, women, and children inside the city of Jerusalem in 1099, the Rape of Nanking by Japan in 1937 resulting in 300,000 dead and most women raped, and the slaughter in the Rwandan civil war of nearly a million people in 100 days in 1994. With war unleashing every kind of darkness in people, we can appreciate any effort to limit the effects of war.

3. Christian just war theory arose because people were aware at a glance that taking weapons and using them to end the lives of others flies in the face of plain statements of Jesus. There is the recognition that engaging in bloody war is at odds with a message that says, "Go, preach the good news to all nations, so everyone can become brothers and sisters in the same spiritual family." In just war theory there is the recognition that Christians need to give serious thought to war before they engage in it and have a reason for not loving the enemy.

Problems for Just War Theory

While we can appreciate certain aspects of the just war approach, I still find some serious deficiencies that need to be examined by disciples who believe they can use it to defend military involvement. Let me describe my concerns:

1. *Christian just war theory cannot apply in our secular nation-states.* Christian just war theory began when church and state were united, and it is primarily formed on the assumption that those who declare war are themselves people concerned about doing God's will and not going outside a godly morality. In today's world, the only theocracies are found in the Muslim world. While they have an interest in doing Allah's will, they take their direction from the Qur'an and not from Jesus. Other nations are secular in nature and make their decisions about war based on legal, economic, diplomatic, and territorial issues. Today's soldiers may trust their leaders and believe they want to act reasonably according

to international law, but they have no reason to believe that the chief decision-makers have considered Christian just war theory before deciding to act. They have no way to be sure that those who declare war want to conduct that war in line with the principles of *jus in bello.*

2. Just war theory comes from an effort to work out a moral question, yes, but *without reference to the teachings of Jesus or the New Covenant Scriptures.* As you read through the defense of just war theory, you find many references to Natural Law, to human reason, to philosophy, and sometimes to the old covenant Scriptures, but almost no references to Jesus or his teachings. The reason seems rather obvious: Jesus and his followers did not see that those in the Kingdom of God would be involved in war. As soon as you turn to the teachings of Jesus, you find much more than "don't use excess force against your enemy." If you are working on just war ideas, Jesus upsets the whole discussion.

3. *Just war is notoriously difficult to define.* Even if we all could agree that there is such a thing as a just war that a Christian can fight in with a good conscience, we would first have to agree on what items belong on the required list, and that would be a challenge. I have sketched out the general approach, but the details keep changing, and different writers and groups have different lists. One PhD dissertation I read in my research had this subtopic: "Overarching Disputes in Contemporary Analytical Just War Theory." As you can well imagine, there were plenty of disputes described.

Even if everyone could agree on the same list of requirements, then there would be many opinions about whether a given situation meets those requirements. The value of the "last resort" idea, of course, is that it provides restraint and discourages what is often an eagerness to rush into war to exact justice. However, it is of little value in determining just when to engage in war, since sincere people will disagree on when the point of last resort is reached.

The United States bombed and invaded Iraq in 2003 and began a war that would last almost eight years and lead to at least 300,000 deaths. This, while many in the international community were pleading for more time for weapons inspectors to do their job.[40] Many believed there were more options and a time of last resort had not been reached. Who can say? This is true of many elements of just war theory. There are so many judgment calls to be made. Who decides that "the means of war will be both discriminative and proportional" or that our "use of arms will not produce evils and disorders graver than the evil to be eliminated"?

Anyone who thinks that we can easily define a just war should read the entry on "Just War Theory" in the Internet Encyclopedia of Philosophy. When one considers all the different approaches, it is no wonder that many conclude that there is simply no way to bring the matter of ethical concerns and apply it to the chaos of war.

4. *There are times when a war will be seen one way at the beginning but seen completely differently at the end.* The American war in Vietnam is a classic example. At the start, the American public saw it as entirely justified to save the world from Communism. By the time the war ended, most people had an entirely different view.

It is now, for the most part, agreed that the U.S. government lied to the American people throughout the war and propped up a corrupt regime in the South, all while dropping seven million tons of bombs on Vietnam, Laos, and Cambodia (more than twice the amount of bombs dropped on Europe and Asia in World War II). Estimated death toll for the war: one million North Vietnamese and Viet Cong soldiers, 200,000 South Vietnamese soldiers, 58,000 U.S. soldiers and as many as two million civilians. We may be told a war is justified, but there are too many things we don't know about what goes on behind the scenes and too many things we won't know until it is all over. By then the soldiers have turned some of their most crucial moral decisions over to someone else and have committed acts that may haunt them for a lifetime.

5. *Individuals do not get to decide if a war is just.* This is a first principle of historic just war theory. The war must be declared by someone in authority. If you are in the military, you must entrust the decisions about war to non-disciples who are over you in the chain of command. There are no Christian nations and no Christian governments, and the only times in history when people thought there were, those governments often went to war with one another. Four hundred years of wars in Europe all between "Christian" nations more than proves that point. When you are in the military, you are committed to fighting a war that somebody has decided should be fought, but you have no way of knowing the real reasons for the war. Wars in our day are primarily initiated by politicians or by dictators. Most of us would not use positive words to describe either group. Yet they are the legitimate authorities

in our world. Should you decide it is not a just war and refuse to fight, you will be court-martialed. No just war theorists ever envisioned that individual soldiers had the right to make these decisions. If the proper authority has decided, then the soldiers' role is to fight.

6. *"Just war" is often an expedient excuse or rationalization.* I do not think this is true in every case, but I see lots of evidence for it. Various writers have described how it can be a window dressing, a smoke screen, and a convenient card to play. Men and women join the military for various reasons. Perhaps they are motivated by tradition (as in coming from a long line of military people) or by patriotism (as in wanting to do something after an event like 9/11) or by practicality (as in, the military is a good career with early retirement options). If war comes, it is easy for the "cultural Christian" to go with the flow and play the just war card when called on to fight and destroy the enemy.

But a disciple must study where such an idea came from and ask if it fits at all with Jesus, the Sermon on the Mount, and the rest of the New Testament. *Gott mit uns* ("God with us") was the phrase on the belt buckles of German soldiers in World War II, and Hitler claimed he was fighting a just war because they had been attacked by Poland. The just war card is convenient and easy to play…and so often abused.

7. *Just war theory is almost always…just that, a theory—a theory in the negative sense of the word.* Theory, as in unproved assumption; conjecture. Theory as in speculation. High standards are imbedded in it, and with those lofty standards,

war is initiated. But once it is underway, it is very often a different story. I have not been able to determine when the word "theory" was added to the just war discussion, but the more you examine it, the more you see that this is an appropriate term. Theory is often far from reality.

Let's think of the two world wars of the twentieth century. Nearly everything about World War I is confusing. What was originally called The Great War resulted in the deaths of 8.5 million military personnel and probably another 10 million civilians. It has been called the "utterly useless war" and "the completely avoidable war." There is still no clear answer to the question of who started it or if anybody can be said to have started it. Historians continue to debate what it was really about. The only thing that seems clear is that it was a four-year-long tragedy, and never "the war to end all war," as it was sometimes called after the fact. Yet millions of men patriotically did their duty, put on their uniforms, and fought for one of forty or fifty different countries—shooting, bayoneting, blowing up, or gassing others who felt they were doing the same thing. Trying to make any determination about just war is maddening.

World War II is usually considered to be exhibit A for a just war. In the American narrative it is often called "the good war." However, the Allied forces sought to bring the war to a close by targeting German and Japanese cities and their civilians. Berlin, Dresden, Tokyo, Hiroshima, Nagasaki, and other cities were hit with carpet bombs, fire bombs and, finally, nuclear bombs, resulting in thousands upon thousands of civilian deaths. In March 1945 a single fire-bomb raid on Tokyo killed almost 100,000 people and burned sixteen square miles. The firestorm was so intense that the city's canals were brought to a boil. Over the next four months, Japan's five largest cities were destroyed with 260,000 civilians killed and as many as thirteen million left homeless. With this action, one of the universally agreed on elements of just war—"no targeting of civilians"—was violated, again and again. A "just war" may be started with no intention of attacking civilians, but as war escalates and the enemy will not stop fighting, justification is found for abandoning this principle. Therefore, there are many who ask, "Has there ever been a just war?" All agree that war is horrible. Once it happens, humans have the need to justify it, but has there ever been more than the "theory" of just war?

While I can affirm the heart behind just war thinking, I still find it sadly lacking. I understand how it came about. I appreciate the effort to limit the effects of war. Surely, we can applaud all efforts to be more moral and humane. However, I find this theory to be based on faulty reasoning and assumptions, open to many interpretations, and easy to abuse. I find that, more often than not, its advocates violate their own principles.

John D. Roth also points out that the doctrine of just war has never prevented a war from breaking out. He puts it this way: "There are no recorded cases in history in which a nation has chosen not to pursue war because the Christians in its government or army made a conscientious decision that a particular conflict did not adequately meet the criteria of a just war. From the perspective of the nation-state, every war in which it chooses to participate is just." "Just war" may very well be a conscience-soothing label that has little impact on decisions that are made.

More importantly for a disciple of Jesus, it fails to embrace the high calling of our Teacher and Lord. This theory is not developed from his teachings or the New Covenant Scriptures, but is based on confidence in man's wisdom. Just war theory does not give us sufficient reason to engage in the kind of violence that Jesus forbids or to forsake the kind of enemy-love he specifically tells us to practice. But remember this: In the face of the military issue, if we do not choose the path of nonviolence and the path of enemy-love, this is our only alternative. It is the best that men have been able to devise, but it is fraught with problems. Above all, it is not the way of the cross.

Our first obligation is to follow Jesus, not to go along with what rulers, democratic or otherwise, have decided. We are talking here about issues of life and death. We are talking about actions that may take another life or thousands of lives. Thankfully, we do not have to rely on the world's wisdom. The Scriptures tell us, "Do not be overcome by evil, but overcome evil with good" (Romans 12:21). With the help of God that is what we can do and will do.

7

THE MILITARY EXPERIENCE

In the United States and generally around the world the military enjoys great popularity. In 2004 Gallup reported that in the U.S., the average confidence level across 14 institutions in society was 43%, but by 2016 that number was down to only 32%. In contrast, confidence in the military remained where it has been for years at about 73%. So, should we really be scrutinizing the element of society that has the greatest respect and approval? Should I be devoting this volume to the disciple and the military when there are so many needs to be addressed? Since so few of us will be in the military, shouldn't we be looking at something that applies to a much larger group of us? To answer these questions, I believe it will help to take a closer look at the experience of the soldier. To do this I will focus on the activities of the foot soldier or those sent into combat. I realize that after basic training many, if not most, in the military go on to other ways of serving, and that most will never see the enemy. However, everyone in uniform must be first trained for war and always ready to enter into it.

In Chapter 1 we looked at character traits (like loyalty, duty, and selfless service) that are often focused on in military training. It is believed that these traits are needed for all that a soldier will be asked to do. However, basic training will focus many hours on how these values are to be lived *in combat*—the soldier must be trained for war.

Learning War

A military person is in the "armed forces," an organization that when called upon, will seek to impose its will on the military of another country through the use of "force." This is true whether the goal is defensive or offensive. Such force is exerted through the use of "arms," meaning weapons designed to kill the enemy and/or destroy the equipment and material of the enemy.

As the soldier is issued a gun, a rifle, a bayonet, or hand grenades, it is obvious to all that the warrior is being *trained to kill the enemy.* He or she will be given careful instruction about just how to do it, and the message will be repeated over and over. Since most people have a natural reluctance to kill, the military will make every effort to train them to overcome that tendency so they can fulfill their mission. As most military leaders will tell you, if the military does not teach recruits to kill, it will be ineffective and might as well fold its tent.

While Jesus could very well support training in loyalty, duty, respect, selfless service, honor, integrity, and personal courage, what would he say about training to kill? Given that Jesus teaches us to do to others as we would have them do to us, how does killing others fit in? Isaiah's vision of kingdom people is that "they will neither harm nor destroy on all my holy mountain" (Isaiah 11:9), but the soldier must be trained to inflict the ultimate harm on the opposing men and women. Doesn't this raise some serious questions? Given Jesus' call for us to love our enemies and do good to them, what kind of training do we most need? Don't all these matters require us, as Jesus' followers, to give special thought to our view of the military?

Perhaps it is surprising, but military leaders, at least these days, understand that many people struggle with killing. Retired Army Lt. Col. Peter Kilner writes often about these issues and addressed the matter while on the faculty of the U.S. Military Academy. He continues to blog on related questions at soldier-ethicist.blogspot.com, which he describes as an online space for thinking about war, morality, and the profession of arms.

The BBC did a story on Kilner's work and reported him saying, "A central part of what we [military people] do with our careers is we kill the enemies of our country. So it's very important that we understand why, and under what conditions it's the morally right thing to do to kill another human being." Killing, he says, creates considerable psychological distress for many soldiers. In his words, "They don't like to talk about it. In general, if you're a soldier and you've killed in war, you lie and say no. It tends to be the secret we have that we're not proud of. We want to fight bravely, but it's hard to be proud of killing another person."

Kilner feels that the military needs to do much more to help soldiers work through their thoughts and feelings about killing others. "We recruit people to kill," he says. "We train people to kill. We make the orders. Yet after the fact, we don't talk about killing. We talk about destroying, engaging, dropping, bagging—you don't hear the word 'killing.'" But it is his belief that soldiers struggle with what may feel is a morally ambiguous action, and they need to be helped to understand (in his thinking) it was the right thing to do.[42]

In an interview with PBS, Kilner was asked his view regarding desensitizing and automatic stimulus response training. Most of us would ask, what is this referring to? To give the answer requires some background.

After World War II a famous study was done by S.L.A. Marshall, the official U.S. Army historian of that war. Amazingly, he found that on average no more than 20% of combat soldiers fired their weapons in battle and that a significant number who did fire, fired over the heads of the enemy. Marshall eventually wrote that "fear of killing, rather than the fear of being killed, was the most common cause of battle failure in the individual." Questions have been raised about some of Marshall's methodology or his exact results, but the Army accepted his general conclusion that troops were most reluctant to kill another human being.

With information from Marshall's study, the Army began to use methods in basic training to enable men to overcome their innate (or is it God-given?) resistance to killing.

One of these was *desensitization,* a process where you get the soldier used to the idea of killing so it begins to feel normal. Sometimes repetitive bloodthirsty language is employed. One example: "You want to ruin and destroy (the enemy) and send him home in a Glad bag to his mommy." To maximize desensitization, this kind of language is used repetitively. Various efforts are made to depict the enemy as "subhuman" or "inhuman." The reasoning: The more you can deny their humanity and think of them as animals, the easier it will be to kill them.

Another method is operant conditioning (you might think of Pavlov's dog, but this is a more refined method that comes from B.F. Skinner). Here the person is exposed to various stimuli (like pop-up targets on the shooting range) and is rewarded or punished based on their response, e.g., how quickly they fire and hit the (human looking) targets. A trainee spots the targets, fires almost on instinct, and gets rewarded with points, badges, and three-day passes. Over and over, these "kill drills" build muscle memory and acclimate the brain to the act of killing. The idea is that when faced with the enemy, the soldier won't be trying to sort things out morally, but just reacting according to the new conditioning.

Another method focuses on training in close combat, with the idea that if one can get used to killing "up close," then it will be all the easier to kill someone 100 yards away with a rifle. One U.S. Army publication found on the internet has an article from a training manual titled: "The Personal Nature of Killing" by Clete Goetz 642nd EN CO, 548th CSB, 10th MTN DIV. In part it reads:

> Killing someone becomes more difficult as the means of their demise becomes more personal. For example, strangling or stabbing someone is more abhorrent psychologically to the average person than shooting someone through open sights. Incorporating combatives, knife-fighting techniques, take-downs, etc., *will help to create killers.* If you can train soldiers to stab someone, you can expect them to shoot the enemy when required. You must create the mindset in them that killing the enemy is an acceptable action when done in obedience to the governing authority (emphasis added).[43]

And, finally, resistance to killing is overcome through an older but still useful method known as propaganda, which involves repeatedly telling trainees how the enemy wants to destroy "our" way of life or take away our freedom or bind their beliefs and values on us, etc.

The U.S. military believes their methods have been successful, with shooting rates rising through the Korean War, and eventually getting to 90% by the end of the Vietnam War. However, as we will see, the military may be reporting better statistics, but despite these methods and techniques, there are still many who are profoundly disturbed by their experience of killing.

Are the Methods Moral?

But let's get back to Lt. Col. Kilner. How did he reply when asked about desensitizing and automatic stimulus response training? The interviewer was obviously wanting his thoughts about the morality of such methods. You can read the whole interview yourself on the POV/PBS website, but Kilner seems to be quite conflicted.[44]

On the one hand, he believes this training may be needed, and useful in saving the lives of our troops, but on the other hand, he is not so sure it is best to dehumanize the enemy. Here is his actual reply: "So I think that rather than ignoring the issue, pretending it's not human beings that you're killing, but recognizing their full humanity, recognizing that, hey, based on their choices this is what they get, maybe at the moment it'll be a little more upsetting, but in the long term I think it'll be much healthier for the people involved."

I think what he is saying is that in the short run, it is more upsetting to face the fact that you are killing another human being, but in the long run it is best, because eventually you are going to have to think about what you did, and it is healthier not to deceive yourself at any point along the way.

As the interview goes on, you can still sense Kilner's struggle. On the one hand, he says the military must move toward these reflexive fire techniques, because "we want our soldiers—these are the people that are defending our freedoms—to be faster and more lethal than the enemy." But then he adds, "What we'll do reflexively—you know, at some point you're going to reflect on it, whether it's two hours later, two weeks later, or two decades later."

Then we see what Kilner has settled on as the main goal: "It's sense-making," he says. He feels the military owes it to the troops to help them sit down after the fact and make sense of what they have done. He doesn't object, for the most part, to the methods used to prepare them, if they are given help in making sense of what they did, by which he seems to mean seeing that it was moral for them to kill in those circumstances. In other words, that the end justifies the means. Kilner goes on to admit to his interviewer that after the fact you will sometimes realize that in the heat of the action you did the wrong thing, and say to yourself, "Yup, if I'd thought about it I would have done the right thing, but if I had thought about it, I might [also] have gotten killed."

My point here is that even for nonbelievers and non-disciples, training to kill and then actually killing other people brings up moral struggles, psychological disturbances and ambiguities. If that is true, how much greater should the struggle be for those who have been called to a much higher standard because they have been born anew into the Kingdom of God? How much more thought do we need to give to this? How much more concern must we have about doing the right thing *in the first place* and not just making some sense of our actions after the fact? How much more do we need to question whether the end ever justifies the means?

I appreciate those like Kilner who wrestle with moral issues, but disciples of Jesus are called to God's will on earth as it is in heaven, to hold out a light into a dark world, not just to be able to make sense of carnage after they have obeyed orders to kill.

Team Work, the Chain of Command, and the Enemy

But let's consider another aspect of training before we move on to the experience of the soldier. As soldiers learn to use their weapons, they must also learn to use their weapons in tandem and coordination with others. Seldom, if ever, will a soldier operate as a Lone Ranger. Few are chosen for sniper duty.

Soldiers must learn to operate as a team, and consequently, the function of the army will be based on discipline and strict obedience to those over you. Every soldier must be trained to rapidly carry out the orders which he or she receives. The chain of command is expressed by the military rank system and hierarchy, and must always be followed. Soldiers must obey superior officers. As the former Navy pilot told me, "The point of training is that the military person will react quickly and accurately. The primary problem in questioning a command is the delay involved, which is *why training so emphasizes not to question* (emphasis added)."

But here is the quandary. In the United States military, when it comes to obeying orders, there is only one exception: *orders which are illegal,* particularly those which violate human rights or international law, must not be obeyed. To do so may be considered a war crime. However, in most circumstances, when someone in authority over you says, "That is the enemy. Kill him," or "Kill her," it is the job of the soldier to obey. Deciding on the spot in the heat of the moment that some order is an "illegal order" takes the ordinary soldier into an arena they usually feel is far above their pay grade. In the words of my Navy veteran: "Running each order through a filter of 'legality' causes delays that get people killed." Those in the military are more likely to agree with Tennyson, who wrote of the 600 in the Light Brigade, "Theirs not to reason why | Theirs but to do and die." Following World War II, many German soldiers rationalized atrocities by saying they were only following orders.

This training and expectation to obey orders brings up a real dilemma for the disciple of Jesus. In the first place, to be in the military means you have surrendered a significant portion of your own moral decision-making to someone in authority over you. One can hope those officers have some legitimate moral code, but that will depend on what country we are talking about and the individual officer. However, we can be sure that even in the best of circumstances, the Jesus-standard will be higher than any moral code a superior is following. So it would not be surprising for a soldier to be given orders that conflict with obedience to Jesus. I know of no military force that pledges to follow the Sermon on the Mount.

However, even if the entire chain of command holds to a very high standard, there will always be one critical issue: your superiors will define for you who is the enemy and what you are to do to that enemy. If you are a follower of Jesus in Russia, the enemy might be defined for you as the United States or the NATO countries of Europe. If you are in the United States, the enemy might be defined for you as China or Russia or North Korea or some other country that an unconventional American president happens to not like. The point is if you are in the military, the government tells you who is the enemy.

Your superiors will talk often about the enemy. Normally they will vilify and demonize the enemy. They may encourage you to hate the enemy. Three-star General Leslie McNair was the highest-ranking U.S. servicemember to die in World War II. Preparing his troops, General McNair famously said:

> Our soldiers must have a fighting spirit; if you call that hating enemies, then we must hate with every fiber of our being. We must lust for battle; we must scheme and plan night and day to kill; we must hit harder and harder; we must become tougher and tougher; the avowed purpose of the army is to make killers out of every soldier.[45]

Ironically, General McNair was killed by *friendly* fire on July 25, 1944.

Legendary documentary maker Ken Burns completed a series of programs on the Vietnam War that was released in the fall of 2017.

General McNair's words remind me of the comments of a soldier from Fairmont, Missouri, featured in that series. "You go to war with one mindset, but then you adapt. You adapt to the killing...to the bodies and then it doesn't bother you. I should say it doesn't bother you as much." And then he added, "My hatred for them [the enemy] was pure. I was so scared of them and the more scared I was, the more I hated them. To stay sane and do your work as a soldier, you have to turn the enemy into objects. You can't think of them as human beings."[46]

G. K. Chesterton once wrote: "The true soldier fights not because he hates what is in front of him, but because he loves what is behind him." The military apparently cannot agree with such an optimistic view. Hating the enemy is often seen as necessary. The goal of the military is to win battles and win wars. We expect them to take a certain view of the enemy and to get their men and women to feel a certain way about the enemy. They know how dangerous it is to have a generous attitude toward your foes.

Perhaps you have heard of the Christmas ceasefire during World War I. The story has been retold many times and frequently embellished, but something did happen that is noteworthy and instructive. On December 7, 1914, four months into the conflict, Pope Benedict XV suggested a temporary hiatus of the war for the celebration of Christmas.

The warring countries refused to create any official ceasefire, but on Christmas Eve at a few places across the Western Front, German and British soldiers in the respective trenches began to sing Christmas carols. Eventually they were singing them back and forth to one another. On Christmas day some of the Germans emerged into no-man's-land and greeted the British, calling out "Merry Christmas." Overcoming their suspicion, some of the British finally came out, where there was handshaking and the exchange of gifts, like cigarettes and plum pudding. There are reports of carol singing together, and that someone brought out a football (soccer ball to Americans) and while there was no organized game, as is sometimes said, apparently the opposing sides enjoyed kicking it around. The next day they were back to the business of war, giving all their efforts to killing one another.

For some, this offered hope that in a brutal war, man's humanity could still be seen. For others it was a reminder that the average folks generally don't have anything against one another, they are just fighting to carry out some leaders' agenda. However, to the high command on both sides, this incident was most disturbing. It brought a harsh rebuke and strong warnings that it should never be repeated. *No decent treatment of the enemy was to be tolerated.* The generals understood how damaging this could be to the prosecution of the war. They announced that anyone who engaged in this going forward would be court-martialed. They knew that the more you humanize the enemy, the less chance you have of defeating them.

But Jesus says, "You have heard that it was said, 'Love your neighbor and hate your enemy.' But I tell you: Love your enemies and pray for those who persecute you." Jesus' message and example teach us to treat every human being as one made in the image of God. That means the last thing we ever want to do is dehumanize them. Instead we want to see the soul and divine potential in everyone.

There is the world's wisdom and there is God's wisdom.

Moral Injury

One of the biggest topics in military circles these days is that of "moral injury." Although, at this writing, it is not officially recognized by the U.S. Department of Defense, "moral injury" does appear on Veterans Administration websites where it is defined and discussed.[47] The term was first used by psychiatrist Jonathan Shay in 1994. Most everyone is familiar with post-traumatic stress disorder (PTSD), which refers to the mental and emotional stress one suffers as a result of injuries and shocking experiences, often in war. But more and more experts are seeing moral injury, the pain that results from damage to a person's moral foundation, as just as serious.

The fact that U.S. military veterans have been committing suicide at a rate of twenty a day for quite some time has caused military leaders and mental health professionals to look at both of these issues as likely factors. Some are even describing moral injury as the signature wound of this generation of veterans.

So, what is a moral injury? It is variously described as:

- A bruise on the soul, akin to grief or sorrow.
- A sense that what is right has been greatly violated.
- The result of intentionally doing something that you felt was against what you thought was right.
- Disruption in an individual's confidence and expectations about one's own or others' motivation or capacity to behave in a just and ethical manner.
- The inability to contextualize or justify personal actions or the actions of others and the unsuccessful accommodation of these experiences into preexisting moral schemas.
- A deep soul-wound that pierces a person's identity, sense of morality, and relationship to society.

Although a moral injury can manifest with symptoms similar to those seen in PTSD, such as acts of avoidance, intrusive thoughts, numbness, and loss of interest in activities, those who have sustained a moral injury also often feel extreme shame or guilt for acts they have committed or witnessed in combat.

Retired Lt. Col. Kilner, in a memorable blog post, writes the following:

> Moral injury is the psychological, social, and/or spiritual harm that results from experiencing a violation of a deeply held moral belief, perpetrated by a trusted authority, in a high-stakes situation such as war.
>
> The "trusted authority" who betrays and loses that trust can be:
>
> 1. The soldier, when he/she does something that violates their own moral code.
> 2. A leader (or entire chain of command), when he/she disregards the humanity of the soldier.
> 3. God, or the soldier's sense of the divine, when the soldier encounters senseless, unfair suffering.[48]

Shira Maguen, a staff psychologist at the VA Medical Center in San Francisco, has done extensive research into moral injury, particularly by doing hours of interviews with Vietnam veterans. Military leaders were not pleased with her conclusion that *moral injury is sustained by soldiers in the course of doing exactly what their commanders and society ask of them.* She concluded that it is not necessary for one to witness atrocities or some of the greater horrors of war to sustain a moral injury, but it occurs in the "normal" conduct of war.[49]

Moral injury and PTSD have their similarities, but moral injury particularly manifests itself in the following:

- Shame (for example "I am an evil, terrible person; I am unforgivable.")
- Guilt
- Anxiety about possible consequences
- Anger about betrayal-based moral injuries
- Social instability
- Withdrawal and self-condemnation
- Self-harming (e.g., suicidal thinking and attempts)
- Self-handicapping behaviors (e.g., alcohol or drug use, self-sabotaging relationships, etc.)

Civilian Deaths

Those who study moral injury make two points: (1) Those involved in killing are at higher risk of moral injury than those who are not. (2) Those who are involved in civilian deaths are even more likely to suffer from moral injury. Although most countries say they are committed to avoiding such civilian deaths, vast numbers of civilians die in every war and are euphemistically referred to as "collateral damage." According to Graça Machel in the UN Secretary-General's office, civilian fatalities in wartime climbed from 5% at the turn of the twentieth century, to 15% during World War I, to 65% by the end of World War II, to more than 90% in the wars of the 1990s.[50]

What this means is that there is a high probability that soldiers involved in war will be involved in the deaths of civilians; and such incidents are significant contributors to moral injury. Anyone going into the military must face this fact.

New York Times writer, Eyal Press, attended a support group for soldiers recovering from moral injury. That night he heard from a man identified as "Andy," who told of being on a mission in the Sunni Triangle when he thought the enemy was firing from a house. Andy called for an airstrike. When the smoke cleared something else was revealed. In his own words: "I see instead the wasted bodies of nineteen men, eight women, nine children. Bakers and merchants, big brothers and baby sisters. I relive this memory almost every day. I confess to you this reality in the hope of redemption, that we might all wince and marvel at the true cost of war." Eyal Press reports, "The room fell silent as Andy went back to his chair, sobbing."[51]

Daniel Somers was a veteran of Operation Iraqi Freedom with an impressive military resume. He was part of Task Force Lightning, an intelligence unit. In 2004–2005, he was mainly assigned to a Tactical Human-Intelligence Team (THT) in Baghdad, Iraq, where he ran more than 400 combat missions as a machine gunner in the turret of a Humvee, interviewed countless Iraqis ranging from concerned citizens to community leaders and government officials, and interrogated dozens of insurgents and terrorist suspects. In 2006–2007, Daniel worked with Joint Special Operations Command (JSOC) through his former unit in Mosul where he ran the Northern Iraq Intelligence Center. His official role was as a senior analyst for the Levant (Lebanon, Syria, Jordan, Israel, and part of Turkey).

On June 10, 2013, Daniel wrote a final letter to his family before taking his life. Daniel was thirty years old. His wife and family gave permission for it to be published. It went viral.

In it he said, "During my first deployment, I was made to participate in things, the enormity of which is hard to describe. War crimes, crimes against humanity.… These things that go far beyond what most are even aware of. How can I possibly go around like everyone else while the widows and orphans I created continue to struggle?"⁵²

As I was in the latter stages of writing this book, news broke that in the war in Yemen an airstrike launched by U.S.-backed Saudi forces struck a school bus with children returning from camp. The news footage showed ten-and eleven-year-olds with bloody heads and bleeding legs, but did not show thirty other little boys who were killed in the strike.⁵³

Joystick Warriors

One of the major changes the twenty-first century has brought to warfare has been the introduction of drones. The first U.S. "kill" by a drone was in 2001 in Kandahar Province, Afghanistan. Now it is a major weapon in the U.S. arsenal. Recently a *New York Times* reporter visited Creech Air Force Base in Nevada, the home of 900 drone pilots who fly lethal aircraft over Afghanistan, Pakistan, Yemen, and other theaters. From that base and other sites it is estimated that these men and women have used drones to kill more than 10,000 people including as many as 1500 civilians.

The *Times* article reports the surreal work of drone pilots this way:

> One minute they are at war; the next they are at church or picking up their kids from school. A retired pilot, Jeff Bright, who served at Creech for five years, described the bewildering nature of the transition. "I'd literally just walked out on dropping bombs on the enemy, and 20 minutes later I'd get a text—can you pick up some milk on your way home?"

One might think that personnel involved in combat in such a remote way would be nearly immune to the trials of PTSD or moral injury. But the reporter reveals in a remarkable article that this certainly is not the case. He describes it this way:

> Far from exhibiting a sense of carefree detachment, three-fourths reported feeling grief, remorse and sadness.... According to another recent study conducted by the Air Force, drone analysts in the "kill chain" are exposed to more graphic violence—seeing "destroyed homes and villages," witnessing "dead bodies or human remains"—than most Special Forces on the ground.[54]

He found life was not so easy for what he called joystick warriors. To help these remote-control soldiers, the military embedded with them a group of physiologists, chaplains, and psychologists called the Human Performance Team. What we learn from the *Times* report is that you can live in the Las Vegas suburbs, commute forty-five minutes to work, do your military job, pick your kids up from sports, have dinner with the family, and suffer terribly from a moral injury.

One servicemember from Colorado described his experience this way: "When you have nightmares every night, and those moments are replayed in your face, and you wake up with your bed full of sweat and a wife who looks at you like you're crazy. Those are the moments I regret. I regret going home after a strike and pretending that I was okay at my daughter's birthday party."

If you happened to see the film *Eye in the Sky* starring Helen Mirren, you were given a realistic view of the lives of drone operators and the dilemmas they can face.

As enlightening as the *Times* article was, the letters the paper received from soldiers in response were even more striking. Here are some of those. I have deleted surnames.[55]

> I saw firsthand the many ways in which we brutalize and kill our fellow humans. I recoiled, but then I began to feel those same urges within myself. It sickened me, but I came to accept that this is who we are and this is what we do. Naturally, this is not a subject for polite conversation. But moral injury is a real thing. It's the shock of realizing who I am. (Chet ___, Little River, Calif.)

> I didn't recognize myself in the mirror, and I suffered from digestive issues and difficulty sleeping. I also suffered from depression and suicidal ideation. While I was deployed, my young cousin thanked me for keeping him safe, but I couldn't bring myself to respond for fear of lying. When I returned, I didn't believe that I was a good person and identified with the lines from the film "Road to Perdition": "This is the life we chose, the life we lead. And there is only one guarantee: None of us will see heaven." Because of this impression, I had a general sense of disconnect from the people around me. I came to understand that I suffered from moral injury through a combination of values-based therapy and my reading on the subject. Although an ongoing process, I am finally reconciled with who I am. (Sean ___, Cambridge, Mass.)

> Onset of extreme anxiety, depression, panic attacks, misunderstood fears, patterns of alcohol abuse. I have never been given a diagnosis of moral injury, only depression. I realized my internal conflict after watching drone strikes during a

> yearlong deployment supporting operations. I started to wonder why most people celebrated the death of another human being. I still feel sick inside over it. (Jeffrey ___, Millersville, Md.)

> I am forever changed. Moral injury is similar to the effect of a cold-weather injury. Once received, the person is forever changed and forever vulnerable to the conditions and circumstances that started it all. A person with frostbite is always vulnerable to cold. A soldier with a wounded heart is always torn by the moral conditions of war, conflict and crisis. (Timothy ___, Dover, Ark.)

I have not written this final section of the chapter to say that disciples should avoid military service because of moral injury. I believe that there are other strong reasons to make that decision. Plus, Christians should not shirk from something simply because it is dangerous. I have, however, written it to say that the significant presence of moral injury shows that war is an environment that greatly challenges the moral underpinnings of men and women. It puts them in situations where there will be tremendous pressure to compromise something in their core. In spite of all the military's efforts to prepare one for killing (using methods that we must question), it seems there is something about that experience that still profoundly disturbs the person who does it. As one writer put it, there is something about training for and engaging in war that is "soul-killing."

I want to conclude this chapter by going back to the questions we started with: Should we really be scrutinizing that element of society that has the greatest respect and approval? Should I be devoting this volume to the disciple and the military, when there are so many

Kingdom-related issues to be addressed? Since so few of us will be in the military, shouldn't we be looking at something that applies to a much larger group of us?

First, just because something has great approval, even respect, in our culture or society, is never a reason for followers of Jesus to naively accept it. Jesus brought a countercultural message. As disciples we must look carefully at the military precisely because it is so revered by our society. We must look behind its reputation, seeing how people are trained and what they are expected to do; we must lay those things beside the Beatitudes and the Sermon on the Mount and be discerning.

Second, I would say we are justified in this inquiry because among my readership there has been very little said about these matters. There has been a fear that too much discussion would result in division, and so some leaders have quietly discouraged a close examination. However, when we have avoided a topic, that is usually all the more reason to look at it and ask "Why?"

Third, there is the issue about few of us being in the military. That is quite true. However, many, if not most, readers of this book live in the United States of America, a country that is variously respected, feared, or reviled because of its military power. And, at the same time, we often support with a certain degree of pride our country's military.

The United States military budget four years ago was $610 billion. (The U.S. president asked for $686 billion for 2018.) Second to the U.S. was China with $216 billion. The United States has 4% of the world's population, but we spend 34% of all the money spent worldwide on military expenses. If you list the eight countries that spend the most on the military, the U.S. spends more than the other seven *combined,* and Americans, for the most part, are proud of what we have and celebrate the military. While Congress gets an approval rating of 15% or lower in most polls, the military consistently scores around 85% with even higher ratings from evangelical Christians.

But ask those in other countries, "Is the United States militaristic?" and most would say yes. All over the world other countries often view the United States, in the words of one magazine, as "an arrogant bully, reserving for itself the right to rain down death from above on anyone it pleases whenever it pleases."[56] This may seem unfair, but it is likely the way much of the world views us. In fact, a 2013 Gallup Poll conducted in sixty-five countries asked this question: Which country do you see as the greatest threat to peace in the world today? The overwhelming winner was the United States.[57]

Yet many of us who are disciples support with pride our military force and culture even if we are not in it. In this situation, it seems only right to examine that culture and ask, "Are we being conformed to the pattern of this world or being transformed by the renewing of our minds?" (Romans 12:2). Are we unequally yoking ourselves with unbelievers? (2 Corinthians 6:14). Yes, the military is respected at home and emphasizes certain values, but are they the values of the Kingdom of God? Do they involve the "more than others" of the Sermon on the Mount?

In discipling others to Jesus, I know many of us carefully counsel people to help them avoid situations that will tempt them to stray from God's call. If a person becomes a disciple of Jesus and works in an environment where they are constantly pressured to engage in unrighteous behavior, we likely encourage them to make a change. But shouldn't we also apply this thinking to even highly respected areas—like the military? When a soldier becomes a disciple, is it not true that this profession is going to make it much more difficult for him or her to wholeheartedly love the enemy or to do to others (especially to the enemy) as we would have done to us? As he or she prays "lead us not into temptation," is it not true that their very assignment and mission may be to do something that is at cross-purposes with the way Jesus lived? Do we not want to encourage people to avoid all kinds of situations like that? Does the fact that the military is highly respected change anything?

These may be tough questions for us. In fact, I know they are very tough for many of us. However, Jesus trains us to always love our enemies and do good to them, while the military trains us, when necessary, to kill our enemies. So the questions must be asked, and faced with humility and openness…and a complete yielding to God and the "foolishness" of his wisdom.

When it comes to using violence to harm others, I can find only one sure place to stand and that is to show kingdom love, Jesus love, to everyone…without exception.

8
GOOD QUESTIONS

While this book represents what I believe is a strong case for disciples of Jesus to take a nonviolent stance and to see that it is not their role to be in military service, I fully understand that legitimate questions are raised by this conviction. No doubt some of those are in the minds of many of you right now.

But let me be clear: We should not hold to any faith conviction because we can give logical answers to every question that can be asked about it. We should hold those convictions because we have compelling reasons to do so, even when we cannot answer every question. I cannot answer every question about the resurrection of Jesus from the dead, but for a whole host of reasons I believe it to be true. I can say that about a number of my own deepest convictions.

However, I believe I should answer as many questions about this issue as I can. I would agree with Stanley Hauerwas, who writes:

> Nonviolence is not a stance that is to be limited to being against war, but rather nonviolence requires that every aspect of our lives be open to listening to those who differ from us. That means that those who are not committed to nonviolence should find their objections to nonviolence fairly represented by [those who disagree with them].[58]

I want to take seriously the questions or objections that people sincerely have in response to what I am saying. In each case, I will attempt to accurately describe the concern others have, while giving my own response. I am in agreement with John D. Roth, who has written:

> The humility of respectful dissent calls Christian pacifists to listen carefully to the concerns raised by their opponents. It calls for a sensitivity in language and tone that can appropriately shift from the bold and prophetic to the gentle and pastoral.[59]

With this in mind, let's look at ten of the most frequently asked questions. I will start with what I consider the easiest objections to answer and work my way toward the more difficult ones, ending with what I consider the toughest question, at least for me.

1. What about the violence and wars of the Old Testament?

On hearing a case for enemy-love, nonviolence, and pacifism, this is often the first objection raised. Anyone with a basic knowledge of the Hebrew Scriptures knows that there are many stories of wars approved by God and lots of bloodshed found there. One website titled "Every Battle in the Bible" has the biblical references for eighty-eight different battles. Another website, set up to defend the Crusades, begins this way: "Divine Revelation affords the use of violence in certain cases and for just reasons. The Old Testament is replete with examples of legitimate warfare sanctioned by God undertaken by the Jewish people. These examples clearly illustrate that God commanded and allowed the use of violence for a holy purpose." This article goes on to use the Old Testament examples to justify the Crusades.[60]

Historically, this has been the most frequent defense given for Christian warfare. If God authorized war and violence for righteous purposes under the old covenant, then it makes sense he would do so under the new, more important, and final covenant. The biggest problem with this is that it ignores the fact that many things that were valid under the old covenant are no longer so under the new covenant. The Hebrew prophet Jeremiah, in Jeremiah 31, looked forward to the coming of a new covenant:

> "The days are coming," declares the LORD,
> "when I will make a new covenant
> with the people of Israel
> and with the people of Judah.
> It will not be like the covenant
> I made with their ancestors." (vv31-33)

Jesus himself speaks of the new covenant he is bringing with his blood that would be poured out (Luke 22:20), and the writer of Hebrews quotes this text from Jeremiah (Hebrews 8:8–12), affirming that this new covenant has come in Jesus in his Kingdom that we are receiving (Hebrews 12:28), and continues with these words: "By calling this covenant 'new' he has made the first one obsolete; and what is obsolete and outdated will soon disappear'" (Hebrews 8:13).

In Scripture we are not given a "flat theology"—meaning one where the Old Testament message and the New Testament message have the same height or weight or relevance for us today. All Scripture is God's revelation, but the first covenant was preparatory, and certain things happened or were commanded under that covenant to prepare us for the new one that would come simultaneously with the in-breaking of the Kingdom of God. Now things have changed.

- Jesus is the mediator of a new covenant (Hebrews 12:24).
- The sacrificial system has been supplanted (Hebrews 10:10–12).
- The temple has fulfilled its purpose, and the temple is no longer a physical building (1 Corinthians 3:16–17).
- The theocratic nation-state of Israel as the people of God under the old covenant has ended (Hebrews 8:13), so there can be no more wars commanded and endorsed by God.
- With the coming of the Kingdom, the nation-state has been replaced by the church—the new Israel (Galatians 6:16; 1 Peter 2:9) which includes people of all nations (Matthew 28:19).
- The types of wars that old Israel fought are, therefore, over and the new Israel does not train for war anymore (Isaiah 2:4).
- Animal sacrifices, the temple, and the theocratic temporal nation and its wars have all ended.
- The law and the prophets have been fulfilled in Jesus (Matthew 5:17).
- The grace and truth—the kingdom life—that comes through Jesus Christ calls us higher and deeper to a type of love that is far greater (Matthew 5:43–48).

In a striking contrast, we find that while many heroes in Old Testament days used the sword, there is nothing in the New Testament that speaks of one born anew as a disciple of Jesus bearing arms and using them, unless we include Peter's foolish action against the high priest's servant, for which he was rebuked by Jesus (Matthew 26:52; Luke 22:51). Instead there is a new struggle fought only with spiritual weapons (Ephesians 6:10ff), which are specifically said not to be the "weapons of the world" (2 Corinthians 10:4).

We do not offer sacrifices as they did before Jesus came. We do not seek to enforce the 613 commands in the Hebrew Scriptures as they did before Jesus came. And we must not wage war as they did before Jesus came, because the old has been fulfilled and that which is greater has come, teaching us a whole new way. We cannot use the Hebrew Scriptures and the old covenant to justify our use of violence.[61]

2. What about what John the Baptist said to the soldiers? He didn't tell them to leave the military.

You don't read very far into the Gospels until you come to an encounter where John dialogues with the people, including soldiers. Luke records it this way:

> "What should we do then?" the crowd asked.
>
> John answered, "Anyone who has two shirts should share with the one who has none, and anyone who has food should do the same."
>
> Even tax collectors came to be baptized. "Teacher," they asked, "what should we do?"
>
> "Don't collect any more than you are required to," he told them.
>
> Then some soldiers asked him, "And what should we do?"
>
> He replied, "Don't extort money and don't accuse people falsely—be content with your pay." (Luke 3:10–14)

In defending the idea of Christians in the military, some have pointed out that John speaks to these soldiers about repentance, but he does not tell them to resign from the army or put down their swords. If military participation was not right for those in the coming Kingdom, surely John would have called them to take more action than he mentions here.

In response, I have to admit that it seems that he would have gone further. However, we must point out the error in thinking that everything involved in repentance is found in John's replies. If that were the case, the person who gives one of his shirts away could do that and then feel he had met the requirement and be free to hold on to other sins. The tax collector could continue other unsavory practices as long as he didn't collect more than the Romans required him to. Surely, it could not be true that the only behaviors soldiers had to stop were extorting money, falsely accusing people, and griping about their pay. In the Roman army of the time, soldiers were required to flog a fellow soldier when the commander called for disciplinary measures, cut off the hand of deserters, often humiliate the people they defeated, and participate in crucifixions of those deemed to be enemies of the empire. Here is the way the Jewish historian Josephus described one incident:

> The soldiers out of the wrath and hatred they bore the Jews, nailed those they caught, one after one way, and another after another, to the crosses, by way of jest; when their multitude was so great, that room was wanting for the crosses, and crosses wanting for the bodies.[62]

A soldier who disobeyed an order to carry out such actions could be put to death by beheading—and such beheadings would be done by fellow soldiers upon order. Add to this the fact that Roman soldiers were required to participate in idol worship, as we will discuss more in Chapter 9 when we consider Cornelius, the centurion.

Was John saying it was permissible to continue these practices since he didn't mention them? I think we can all see the flaw in that logic. John's words here must be viewed as examples of the kinds of things involved in a new way of living, but we must not think of these as comprehensive lists.

In addition, we must remind ourselves that John's message was preparatory. He was the last of the prophets under the old covenant. His message was hardly complete. As far as we know, John did not teach many things that Jesus would soon teach. He was preparing the way for the Messiah, who would teach fully what the Kingdom of God was about. The decision about whether to be a combat soldier must be made on other grounds, not the silence of this text. There is far too little here for any broad conclusions.

3. What about Jesus' appeal to the sword?

Here is how another objection is raised: If Jesus was so opposed to weapons of violence, why does he make two different statements in which he appears to say a sword is needed? The two references are found in Matthew 10 and Luke 22. Let's examine them both.

Let's look first at the context of the statement in Matthew 10. This chapter begins with the selection and sending out of the twelve apostles. Instructions are given about how they are to conduct themselves and warnings are given about the resistance that they will encounter. In verse 21 we hear Jesus warn that "brother will betray brother to death, and a father his child; children will rebel against their parents and have them put to death. All men will hate you because of me, but he who stands firm to the end will be saved."

After more warnings, we come (in verse 34) to the text regarding the sword:

> "Do not suppose that I have come to bring peace to the earth. I did not come to bring peace, but a sword. For I have come to turn
> 'a man against his father,
> a daughter against her mother,
> a daughter-in-law against her mother-in-law—
> a man's enemies will be the members of his own household.'
> "Anyone who loves their father or mother more than me is not worthy of me; anyone who loves their son or daughter more than me is not worthy of me; and anyone who does not take their cross and follow me is not worthy of me. Whoever finds their life will lose it, and whoever loses their life for my sake will find it." (Matthew 10:34–39)

Given that Jesus is ushering in the peaceable kingdom of Isaiah 2, 9 and 11 and given that he has begun his ministry declaring, "Blessed are the peacemakers, for they will be called children of God," what are we to make of this strong statement: "I did not come to bring peace, but a sword"? At first blush, it sounds as if Jesus is completely contradicting his mission so clearly spelled out in other places. But the context is the key to understanding his meaning.

Jesus is proclaiming a message that will bring people to peace with God and to peace with one another, but the sad truth is that not everyone—in fact, most people—will not receive it well because it calls them to far more than they are willing to do. Most people want the peace that Jeremiah condemned when he wrote, "They dress the wound of my people as though it were not serious. 'Peace, peace,' they say, when there is no peace" (Jeremiah 6:14). Most people want a cheap peace, not a costly one. The challenging message that goes deep will be responded to with hostility. The peace that one experiences in the Kingdom is found only when one becomes poor in spirit, broken, and humble—in other words when one dies to self—but most people will not see how serious the problem is and will resist.

The deep message that could bring them real peace is offensive to them, and family and friends who embrace this message become offensive to them. The message of Jesus becomes a sword; not a sword that slays, but a sword that divides, and not a physical sword at all but a metaphorical one. As one writer puts it: "Thus we come to read Jesus as saying, 'Don't think I came to bring a simple, passive, harmless peace. This gospel is going to mean a turbulent life for you, and it's going to cause profound tensions between you and even those who are closest to you.'"[63]

I think most people can see the metaphorical use Jesus is making of the word "sword," and, honestly, I find very few who would argue for a literal interpretation here that is advocating violence. Jesus is just describing the effect of his message and letting all know that he did not come to put Band-Aids over serious problems.[64]

The second passage, however, is more problematic. We are near the end of Jesus' life and once again he is giving instructions to his apostles. Here is what we read in Luke 22:

> He said to them, "But now if you have a purse, take it, and also a bag; and if you don't have a sword, sell your cloak and buy one. It is written: 'And he was numbered with the transgressors'; and I tell you that this must be fulfilled in me. Yes, what is written about me is reaching its fulfillment."

> The disciples said, "See, Lord, here are two swords."
> "That's enough!" he replied. (Luke 22:36–38)

The problem is obvious: If Jesus is opposed to the violent use of the sword, why does he tell his disciples to sell a cloak in order to buy one? Why does he want to be sure the group is armed as he prepares for the last events of his life?

But we start with noticing that when Jesus learns that they already have two swords, he says that is enough. One thing is obvious: Jesus had no intention of mounting an armed resistance to his arrest. That must be true, because two swords would not be nearly enough, if the intent is to fight off those who are going to come to arrest him. He obviously wants the sword for some other reason.

This conclusion is confirmed because a few hours later Peter draws one of the two swords and cuts off the ear of the high priest's servant, a poor guy named Malchus. Jesus' response in that situation is "Put your sword back in its place…for all who draw the sword will die by the sword" (Matthew 26:52). Luke tells us that just before Peter acted, the disciples said, "Lord, should we strike with our swords?" Jesus' answer? "No more of this!" I have earlier suggested that the two swords belonged to the two Simons—Peter and the Zealot. Jesus did not want either of the two to use them.

The riddle of the sword, I believe, is solved by verses 36–37. Listen again and focus on the italics added:

> He said to them, "But now if you have a purse, take it, and also a bag; and if you don't have a sword, sell your cloak and buy one. *It is written: 'And he was numbered with the transgressors'; and I tell you that this must be fulfilled in me.* Yes, what is written about me is reaching its fulfillment."

It appears that the sole purpose of the sword is to enable the prophecy to be fulfilled which is found in Isaiah 53:12: "And [he] was numbered with the transgressors." Why else does that occur right after Jesus' command to buy a sword? Two swords would be more than enough to justify an accusation that Jesus was leading a band of people up to no good—particularly a group of rebels.

When the disciples say, "See, Lord, here are two swords," Jesus responds, "That is enough," clearly showing he did not intend for them all to be armed. The International Standard Version may get us closer to the meaning, when it renders verse 38b: "He answered them, 'Enough of that!'" Eugene Peterson in The Message is getting at the same idea when he has Jesus saying, "Enough of that; no more sword talk."

Jesus was on his way to lay down his life, and he was not wanting anyone to defend him with swords. This may be a curious passage, but there is no encouragement in it for the use of weapons.

4. What about the clearing of the temple and expulsion of the moneychangers?

Unusually, all four Gospels report this incident. Here is John's account, which includes the most detail:

> When it was almost time for the Jewish Passover, Jesus went up to Jerusalem. In the temple courts he found men selling cattle, sheep and doves, and others sitting at tables exchanging money. So he made a whip out of cords, and drove all from the temple area, both sheep and cattle; he scattered the coins of the money changers and overturned their tables. To those who sold doves he said, "Get these out of here! How dare you turn my Father's house into a market!" (John 2:13–16 NIV1984).

While there is no talk of swords or bloodshed here, the text is often used to say that even with the generally nonviolent Jesus, there were times to make exceptions. This story gives artists like Rembrandt and El Greco an opportunity to paint Jesus in a rage with people furiously trying to avoid the lashes of his whip.

There is no doubt that this incident shows us a reaction from Jesus that we do not see any other time. But we should be careful not to see something that the text does not say. The common conception is that Jesus used the whip he made from the cords *on the people* (and the painters just mentioned encourage that thinking). However, the text does not say that. A careful examination of the Greek syntax shows that he used the whip and "drove all from the temple area, both sheep and cattle," which was the common way to deal with livestock. The NIV, the NRSV, and the NLT versions all translate it this way. That he expelled people from the temple and turned over the tables is clear, but there is no mention of humans being struck.

Jesus is certainly in this moment full of righteous indignation. What was supposed to be a solemn place to draw near to God was turned into a place of corrupt commerce by the very people who were supposed to represent God. He wanted them to feel the heat. His turning over the tables was the very kind of dramatic symbolic action we sometimes see in the Old Testament prophets.

However, the fact that some have used this incident as a justification for war is much more a reflection of our human hearts than that of Jesus. As John Dear has pointed out, "Perhaps we want Jesus to have some trace of violence in order to justify our own violence. We desperately hope he was violent so that we can dismiss his teachings, wage war, and build nuclear weapons without any guilt."[65]

There are important lessons in this temple incident. One of those is that having enemy-love does not mean being passive or timid. Jesus was most certainly neither of those. But the lesson that is not here is that we are justified in using weapons on those we deem to be unrighteous. One would have to do some real hermeneutical straining to come away with that conclusion.

5. What about the warrior Jesus in Revelation 19? And what about Paul's use of military metaphors? Doesn't this communicate approval of the military?

In my research I was surprised how often this apocalyptic picture of Jesus comes up as a defense for Christian involvement in warfare. What surprises me is how eager many people are to take literally a section of Revelation, a book full of symbolism, not unlike modern-day allegorical classics like Tolkien's *Lord of the Rings*. Because of the very nature of Jewish apocalyptic, we need an entirely different hermeneutical approach, and we are on dangerous ground if we are trying to establish any doctrine or position based first on what we find in Revelation.

Yes, in Revelation 19, Jesus is a seen as a victorious rider on a white horse—a common way to way to portray a victorious king. But Jesus is no more a military commander than he is a sheep, even though he is spoken of twenty-seven times in Revelation as "the Lamb." Both are symbolic of different aspects of Jesus, but neither are to be taken literally, although the second of these is the dominant image of Jesus in Revelation.

The sword that the rider has comes from his mouth. Doesn't that tip us off? John sees Jesus' weapon as the word of God, and even says in verse 13 that his name is "the Word of God." The war Jesus is involved in is a spiritual conflict, and the fight is engaged with spiritual weapons, not literal swords, spears, or M-16s.

God is going to destroy evil, but he will do it through the sacrifice of the Lamb. Notice these passages from chapters 12 and 17:

> Then I heard a loud voice in heaven say:
>
> "Now have come the salvation and the power
>   and the kingdom of our God,
>   and the authority of his Messiah.
> For the accuser of our brothers and sisters,
>   who accuses them before our God day and night,
>   has been hurled down."
> They triumphed over him
>   by the blood of the Lamb
>   and by the word of their testimony;
> they did not love their lives so much
>   as to shrink from death. (Revelation 12:10–11)

> They have one purpose and will give their power and authority to the beast. They will make war against the Lamb, but the Lamb will overcome them because he is Lord of lords and King of kings—and with him will be his called, chosen and faithful followers. (Revelation 17:13–14)

The enemy of Christians in Revelation is the Roman Empire, portrayed as the beast and the false prophet. When read carefully, there is nothing in Revelation that encourages Christians to take the sword, or other means that Simon the Zealot would have once used, to fight against the Romans. On the contrary, Christians, armed only with the blood of the Lamb and the word of their testimony, will willingly go to their death.

And here is the focus the Christians are urged to have:
> Whoever has ears, let them hear.
>
> If anyone is to go into captivity
> into captivity they will go.
> If anyone is to be killed with the sword,
> with the sword they will be killed.
>
> *This calls for patient endurance and faithfulness on the part of God's people.* (Revelation 13:9–10, emphasis added)

As God blessed the patient endurance and faithfulness of Jesus, so he will bless them.

In 1861 American Julia Ward Howe took the words of Revelation 19 and used them to fashion what she called "The Battle Hymn of the Republic." Most U.S. citizens know some of the lyrics:

> Mine eyes have seen the glory of the coming of the Lord;
> He is trampling out the vintage where the grapes of wrath are stored;
> He hath loosed the fateful lightning of His terrible swift sword:
> His truth is marching on.
>
> (Chorus)
> Glory, Glory, hallelujah! Glory, glory, hallelujah!
> Glory, glory, hallelujah! His truth is marching on.
>
> I have seen Him in the watch-fires of a hundred circling camps,
> They have builded Him an altar in the evening dews and damps;
> I can read His righteous sentence by the dim and flaring lamps:
> His day is marching on.

> I have read a fiery gospel writ in burnished rows of steel:
> "As ye deal with my contemners, so with you my grace shall deal";
> Let the Hero, born of woman, crush the serpent with his heel,
> Since God is marching on.
>
> He has sounded forth the trumpet that shall never call retreat;
> He is sifting out the hearts of men before His judgment-seat;
> Oh, be swift, my soul, to answer Him! Be jubilant, my feet!
> Our God is marching on.
>
> In the beauty of the lilies Christ was born across the sea,
> With a glory in His bosom that transfigures you and me.
> As He died to make men holy, let us die to make men free,
> While God is marching on.

Howe wrote not to encourage others in spiritual warfare, but to inspire Union soldiers during the American Civil War. She could see Jesus (or maybe God, since she was a Unitarian) as on the righteous side, present "in the watch-fires of a hundred circling camps." She could read "a fiery gospel writ in burnished rows of steel," an obvious reference to using the guns of war to advance a gospel (by which she, as a Unitarian, likely meant the freedom of the slaves). For Howe, the Jesus of Revelation 19, the "Hero," would lead these troops to victory over their rebel brothers, apparently fulfilling Genesis 3:15 where the Coming One will crush the serpent with his heel.

Julia Ward Howe wrote a stirring song (borrowing the tune from the earlier "John Brown's Body"). She creatively appropriated the words from Scripture. She was on the right side of history. She was opposed to a pernicious evil. But she left us with a view of Revelation

19 that has Jesus as a conquering military leader—the one the Jews wanted him to be—instead of the one he was: the Lamb that was slain. In spite of the popularity and longevity of "The Battle Hymn of the Republic," which we still sing in our churches (to my chagrin), I find no argument for war in Revelation 19.[66] Those who want to argue for Christian participation in it will need to go somewhere else. There is a war and there is conflict, but its nature is spiritual, as non-apocalyptic statements like Ephesians 6 make so clear.

※

But that does bring us to the way Paul uses various military allusions, as we see in the following texts:

> Who serves as a soldier at his own expense? Who plants a vineyard and does not eat of its grapes? Who tends a flock and does not drink of the milk? (1 Corinthians 9:7)

> But I think it is necessary to send back to you Epaphroditus, my brother, co-worker and fellow soldier, who is also your messenger, whom you sent to take care of my needs. (Philippians 2:25)

> Join with me in suffering, like a good soldier of Christ Jesus. No one serving as a soldier gets entangled in civilian affairs, but rather tries to please his commanding officer. (2 Timothy 2:3–4)

> Finally, be strong in the Lord and in his mighty power. Put on the full armor of God so that you can take your stand

against the devil's schemes. For our struggle is not against flesh and blood, but against the rulers, against the authorities, against the powers of this dark world and against the spiritual forces of evil in the heavenly realms. (Ephesians 6:10–12)

> Paul, a prisoner of Christ Jesus, and Timothy our brother,
> To Philemon our dear friend and fellow worker—also to Apphia our sister and Archippus our fellow soldier—and to the church that meets in your home. (Philemon 1:1–2)

Of course, the question here is this: If the military is not for disciples, why does Paul use these terms so positively? My response is three-fold:

1. Illustrations and metaphors are chosen to give hearers something to which they can easily relate. The first-century world was a militarized one. The presence of the Roman soldiers was ubiquitous. These terms were accessible to many and easily understood.

2. Like soldiers engaged in warfare, Christians are engaged in a great struggle. We are representing the invasion of another kingdom into this world. There will be difficulty and resistance, persecution and hardship. We will be viewed as aliens and strangers. But the war will rage not just on the outside but also within ourselves. Certain qualities of soldiers (like those discussed in Chapter 1) will be needed by disciples of Jesus—especially loyalty to our commanding officer, a spirit of obedience, and a willingness to sacrifice.

3. Paul is careful to clarift that the warfare he is talking about is

entirely different. Analogies, metaphors, and illustrations are useful to an extent, but the speaker or writer must take care to be clear in what he or she means and does not mean, if it is not obvious. This Paul does:

- "For though we live in the world, we do not wage war as the world does" (2 Corinthians 10:3).
- "The weapons we fight with are not the weapons of the world. On the contrary, they have divine power to demolish strongholds" (2 Corinthians 10:4).
- "For our struggle is not against flesh and blood, but against the rulers, against the authorities, against the powers of this dark world and against the spiritual forces of evil in the heavenly realms" (Ephesians 6:12).
- Our weapons are truth, righteousness, the gospel of peace, faith, salvation, and prayer (Ephesians 6:13ff).

There is something for the Christian that is analogous to military personnel because both are involved in battle, but I hear Paul making it clear that the object of the warfare, the enemies we face, and the weapons we use could not be more different. The only sword for the Christian to use is the sword of the Spirit, which is the word of God. Paul made it clear enough that for two hundred fifty years after he wrote, no Christian leader understood it any other way.

9

BETTER QUESTIONS

6. Since Romans 13 says that the government is of God and that we are to be subject to the government, wouldn't it be right to support the government when it has decided that military action is necessary?

This is a frequent question and one deserving a good answer. Let me begin with several ideas:

1. The relationship of the disciple of Jesus and God's kingdom to government is a topic that could fill a whole book—and has, several times over. We cannot cover it all here.

2. The topic under consideration in Romans 13 is the authority of government to operate a justice system and punish those who break laws. *International conflicts and wars are not Paul's concern here.* However, because governments often use conscription, or a draft, individuals are sometimes confronted with an ethical decision regarding international disputes that lead to war.

3. Romans 12 and 13 must be kept together. This is crucial. Failure to do so leads to a misreading of chapter 13. In Romans 12, we find the call of the disciple to live out the new age. In Romans 13:1–7 we find how the Christian is to relate to the government as it exercises some control and promotes restraint in the present age (with its "old" ways). Romans

13:8–14 comes back to the role of the Christian who is not conforming to this present age.

Following up on this last point, in the HCSB we notice that Romans 12:1–2 begins with the call for Christians to offer their "bodies" (Greek: *soma*) as a living sacrifice and to not be conformed to the pattern of this "age" (Greek: *aion*). Paul knows that believers are to live by the standards of the age to come and not let this age "squeeze you into its own mould" (Romans 12:2 PHILLIPS).

After addressing the way they are to function as the body of Christ, he then (v17ff) addresses how they are to interact, especially, with those outside the body:

> *Do not repay anyone evil for evil.* Be careful to do what is right in the eyes of everyone. If it is possible, as far as it depends on you, live at peace with everyone. *Do not take revenge, my friends, but leave room for God's wrath,* for it is written: "It is mine to avenge; I will repay," says the Lord. On the contrary:
> "If your enemy is hungry, feed him;
> if he is thirsty, give him something to drink.
> In doing this, you will heap burning coals on his head."
> *Do not be overcome by evil, but overcome evil with good.*
> (Romans 12:19–21, emphasis added)

This defines the attitude of the Christian toward enemies and wrongdoers. Of course, it echoes what Jesus taught about enemy-love in the Sermon on the Mount. Now look at what is said immediately after this about government:

> Let everyone be subject to the governing authorities, for there is no authority except that which God has established. The authorities that exist have been established by God. Consequently, whoever rebels against the authority is rebelling against what God has instituted, and those who do so will bring judgment on themselves. For rulers hold no terror for those who do right, but for those who do wrong. Do you want to be free from fear of the one in authority? Then do what is right and you will be commended. For the one in authority is God's servant for your good. But if you do wrong, be afraid, for rulers do not bear the sword for no reason. *They are God's servants, agents of wrath to bring punishment on the wrongdoer.* Therefore, it is necessary to submit to the authorities, not only because of possible punishment but also as a matter of conscience.
>
> This is also why you pay taxes, for the authorities are God's servants, who give their full time to governing. Give to everyone what you owe them: If you owe taxes, pay taxes; if revenue, then revenue; if respect, then respect; if honor, then honor. (Romans 13:1–7, emphasis added).

When we compare this to chapter 12, we notice the contrast between the Christian's role and the role of the authorities.

- Christians are not to engage in vengeance but are to "leave room for God's wrath" (12:19).
- The governing authorities are God's agent of wrath. God uses governing authorities, as he did pagan nations in the Old Testament accounts, to execute his wrath and accomplish his purposes (13:4).

The Christian (as well as the whole body of Christ) and the state, then, have starkly contrasting roles. The state has a role (from God) in maintaining civil order. Governments will not be righteous (we can count on that), but some or any government and authority is better than anarchy. It is the state's role to be an agent of God's wrath when punishment of evildoers is needed. The state will not always be just in fulfilling this role, but it is not for Christians to try to take this power. It is *not* the role of Christians to be agents of God's wrath. On the contrary, they are to overcome evil with good, with that good being done to enemies.

- The state bears the sword,
- The Christian does not.
- God uses the state for one thing, the Christians for another.

While the Christian is called to the laws of the state, and that was taken seriously by the early church, there was another principle that the church lived by in church-state relations. That principle was declared by Peter in Acts 5:29 in response to the authorities' order not to preach: *"We must obey God rather than human beings!"* Whenever the laws or edicts of the state conflicted with the commands of God, the Christian's allegiance was first to God. This is an inviolable principle. Obedience (or submission) to government always has a limit. Referring to additional comments by Peter is his first letter, Justin Barringer observes:

> Our submission to governments is, therefore, to bear witness to Jesus and his Kingdom. Because Peter says that we obey for the Lord's sake, there are parameters within the command. One cannot submit, by obeying for the Lord's sake, to anything that is contrary to the expressed will of God.[67]

However, Christians are not to start a rebellion against this government that they must, in some specific instances, disobey. We are not to physically fight to set up a new government. We are to obey God, whatever the consequences—while remaining submissive to government in every area where we can, including paying of taxes.

In commenting on Romans 13, Martin Luther took another approach, formulating a dualism, where the Christian divides his life into "spiritual" and "secular" spaces. Romans 12, he argues, guides the "inner spiritual man" and Romans 13 guides the "outer man" as he interacts with the state. Thus, the outer man can take a life if the state calls him to war, while the inner man keeps his heart right.[68] It should be stressed that Luther saw the non-resistance that Jesus taught, but believed the survival of his reformation was dependent on the fighting forces of the German princes, so he was looking for a rationale for the Christian to take the sword. The problem is that in Scripture, the disciple is one person—inner and outer combined—who is to offer his whole self to God (Romans 12:1).[69]

Romans 13 addresses the Christian's basic attitude toward government. That basic attitude is to be one of submission, but never to the point of disobeying God. The state is an authority set up to bring order in this age. We must respect that. But the state is always "of this age." It is used by God and is his servant, not because it is committed to him, but in spite of the fact that it operates according to worldly wisdom.

The Christian and the state will still have very different agendas. Christians are part of God's holy nation (1 Peter 2:9), and their real citizenship is in heaven (Philippians 3:20). This means we must use *special* (shall we say, *extreme*) caution in how we relate to whichever worldly nation-state of which we find ourselves to be a part, submitting to government in every way we can, but never yoking ourselves together with it (2 Corinthians 6:14).

Romans 13 closes with a call for the Christians to be a light in a dark world (13:12), loving our neighbor and, therefore, doing "no harm to a neighbor" (13:9c–10). Paul ends with this encouragement: "Rather, clothe yourselves with the Lord Jesus Christ, and do not think about how to gratify the desires of the flesh." Literally, he says, "put on the Lord Jesus Christ." There is no dualism here. Jesus is not one to be "put on" at certain times and "taken off" at others. We are to wear Jesus at all times and to behave as his disciples in every situation. We must never take off our Jesus hat and exchange it for another.

7. What about Hitler and his type? If everyone did what you say Christians should do, wouldn't evil reign on earth?

For some people, this question just ends the discussion. For them, the pacifists simply cannot be right for this reason. I agree it is a challenging question. Let's suppose for a moment that I cannot give a good answer. What if the whole idea of a being a pacifist in regard to war should end up looking like foolishness in the face of such a question? Would that cause you to walk away from everything else we have looked at? I believe the "Hitler" question can be answered, but I think that it is a good exercise to ask if it is a decisive one.

The Hitler question became more than theoretical for one famous writer who was committed to the kingdom message. Dietrich Bonhoeffer wrote his classic *Discipleship* (*The Cost of Discipleship* in America) in the 1930s. In it, he champions nonviolence and enemy-love. Until fairly recently, it has been taught that the Hitler issue was finally too much for Bonhoeffer and that he became part of a plot (though he was a marginal figure) to assassinate the Fuhrer. For this he was arrested, put in a concentration camp and executed. A more recent book questions this traditional telling of the story and insists that Bonhoeffer remained true to his message of nonviolence.[70] Regardless of which is true, the Hitler question is a tough one.

Speaking of a good exercise, let me give you another one. Here are four statements I believe every faithful disciple can make:

1. I am totally committed to letting God be King.
2. God is sovereign over the nations (Psalm 22:28).
3. God's way often looks like foolishness (1 Corinthians 1:18ff).
4. Only a "few" will ever enter the Kingdom of God (Matthew 7:14).

Take a few minutes and look at these and see what answer you think can be given to the "Hitler" question, just considering these four convictions.

※

If you are done with that exercise, let me share my thoughts. First, if number 1 is not true my answer will almost certainly not be satisfying. Without this commitment, one will view everything from a worldly point of view and my answer will make no sense.

Second, if we are confident that God is sovereign over the nations and history, we are not fearful that we will make some mistake that allows evil to reign. We are freed up to just focus on obeying God and trusting his sovereignty. He will deal with the nations. Justice is a top concern of his, and he will execute it righteously. We don't have to try taking his job. Part of what we must say here is that no one knows how God is working in history, unless he chooses to reveal it. However, we know that in the end, he will still be God and his purposes will be fulfilled. Vengeance is his. He will repay. He will deal with the Hitlers, the Pol Pots, and the like.

Third, because some idea (in this case, pacifism) looks like foolishness, that is no automatic argument against it (not in kingdom thinking). The most important events in history sounded like foolishness to one (or more) whom Jesus trained for three years. When the idea of the Messiah on a cross was placed before Peter, he said, "Never!" It seemed beyond foolish. Maybe a relatively modern word captures it: Absurd! But God's way is not our way: "For the foolishness of God is wiser than human wisdom, and the weakness of God is stronger than human strength" (1 Corinthians 1:25).

Fourth, the hypothetical that says, "What if everyone…" is invalid. The truth is *they won't!* Our role is to proclaim the gospel of the Kingdom to all nations and invite everyone to live the future right now on earth, but Jesus told us: "Enter through the narrow gate. For wide is the gate and broad is the road that leads to destruction, and many enter through it. But small is the gate and narrow the road that leads to life, and only a few find it" (Matthew 7:13–14). Those in the Kingdom will always be "few." Those who will trust that God will work through enemy-love and nonviolence will always be "few." There will always be plenty of others who will say, "We must use violence to stop the Hitlers." God will use them if he so chooses. The world will not fall apart if disciples of Jesus don't fight, but it may have no chance of going on if disciples of Jesus do not love.

8. If Christians aren't willing to fight to stop evil tyrants, aren't they just asking someone else to do the tough, dirty work for them? Aren't Christians evading responsibility?

To go on and put it another way, the critic says, "Aren't pacifists asking someone to protect them and protect their freedom to worship and practice their faith while not being willing to risk their own lives to ensure that freedom?" These are tough questions. I certainly understand the strong emotions and even the logic behind them. This issue is one that has been raised at least since the days of Celsus, who was a critic of Christians in the second century. His claim was that since Christians were not willing to defend the empire, they had no claim to being righteous and should not enjoy its privileges.

One can see why those without spiritual understanding might consider Christians to be cowards, freeloaders, those who sponge off others, or worse. In Great Britain during World War II, conscientious objectors were called "conchies," a pejorative term and one of disgust used to mean all those things. The idea was "Aren't you ashamed to let others fight and die for your freedom while you do nothing?"

Let me make several observations:

1. *This question moves the attention from the words of Jesus* (and Paul) *and focuses on making someone feel shame.* That is not how these issues should be faced nor is it how decisions should be made. If this comes from other believers, they should be reminded that they are not making an appeal from Scripture. Plus, it is more like locker room or street talk and not wrestling with all the texts that we have been considering.

2. *The fact is that Christians do fight against evil.* We just do not fight with the weapons of this world. We seek to overcome evil and to defeat it, but to do that with good, not with more evil. Critics may not recognize or respect our way of fighting, but if we are being obedient to Jesus, we are aligning many forces against evil. Origen in the third century answered

Celsus' criticism this way: "We who by our prayers destroy all demons which stir up wars, violate oaths, and disturb the peace, are of more help to the emperors than those who seem to be doing the fighting." When we fight evil with faith, prayer, and love, we fight with a far greater power than that found in bombs and bullets. In the end, the weakness of God is stronger than human strength.

3. *We must not act to ward off the world's criticism. We must act to please God.* The world, and sometimes other believers, may try to shame us, but we must care more about the approval of God and the way of the cross than about the approval of the world. Peter had some clear words for those who were being ridiculed because of their obedience:

> But even if you should suffer for what is right, you are blessed. "Do not fear what they fear; do not be frightened." But in your hearts set apart Christ as Lord. Always be prepared to give an answer to everyone who asks you to give the reason for the hope that you have. But do this with gentleness and respect, keeping a clear conscience, so that those who speak maliciously against your good behavior in Christ may be ashamed of their slander. It is better, if it is God's will, to suffer for doing good than for doing evil. (1 Peter 3:14–17)

Following Jesus has never been the way of popularity. The world does not give us any medals for our obedience. But that is not our goal. Our goal is to please God by trusting and obeying. If we suffer for doing good, that is the way of the cross.

4. *We don't need soldiers to fight for our freedom in Christ and no war need be fought for that freedom.* Justin Barringer reminds us that there is a great difference in "civic freedom" and freedom in Christ.[71] We can appreciate our civic freedoms and be grateful for them, but we don't need to think that our spiritual freedoms are dependent on having civic ones. Some of us reading this live in countries where we have great civic freedoms. Others of us live in more oppressive situations with fewer freedoms. But regardless of our circumstances we can be free in Christ—free from the power of sin and free to approach God with confidence. Our real freedom can never be given or taken away by the state. Here is how Barringer puts it:

> Christian freedom, true freedom, the freedom that is paradoxically only possible by being bound to Christ, does not come from having an American address or passport or living in a Western-style democracy, and it is not about protecting our rights. It comes from being a citizen of God's now-but-not-yet Kingdom.[72]
>
> […]
>
> True freedom is not having the right to say whatever you want without consequences; it is being able to say what is right regardless of the consequences. Soldiers on battlefields might protect our right to free speech, but the faithful throughout the church's history have retold the story of Jesus in virtually every context, and no threat of imprisonment, torture, or death was able to shut their mouths.[73]

His thoughts remind us of some of those faithful ones in Hebrews 11. As you read this text, ask yourself if they were free.

> Women received back their dead, raised to life again. There were others who were tortured, refusing to be released so that they might gain an even better resurrection. Some faced jeers and flogging, and even chains and imprisonment. They were put to death by stoning; they were sawed in two; they were killed by the sword. They went about in sheepskins and goatskins, destitute, persecuted and mistreated—*the world was not worthy of them* (Hebrews 11:35–38a, emphasis added).

"The world was not worthy of them." Sounds as if they had something special, though they had virtually none of those civic freedoms that we cherish and feel we absolutely need. All these were still waiting for the Messiah who would truly set men and women free, but their faith still brought them a freedom that came from God and not from military victories or legislative action.

There are certainly times when the disciple should be ashamed, but it is not when we refuse to kill. It is when we are embarrassed by the words of Jesus and resort to the violence of the world. It is when we let go of the wisdom of the cross and try to set things right using the world's wisdom. It is when we put the way of Jesus on hold while we yoke ourselves with unbelievers for a season. It is when we decide to do it the Jesus way only *most* of the time.

Those who have decided to say no to violence out of reverence for Christ may be shamed by the world or by fellow believers, but they should never be ashamed. They may be misunderstood and accused, but they should thank God for the grace to continue the way of the cross. Those on that road are no cowards.

Before we go to the next question, let me introduce to you the thinking of Martin L. Cook, who has been a seminary professor, a university philosophy professor, and a professor of military studies at the Army and Navy War Colleges and the Air Force Academy. He lectures often on the morality of war or morality in war. He consistently defends the idea of the Christian in the military, and his main point is related to the question we have currently before us.

In one of his essays, he sums up his argument (designed specifically for Americans) this way:

> All of us in the U.S. benefit from the service of those [in the military] "willing to act" on our behalf. Because they have been so successful for such a long time, we have a luxury that is very rare in human societies. For us citizens, the connection between the peace and prosperity of the society we live in and the reality of our military power is largely invisible to us.
>
> Unless we are really willing to give up the "empire"—the place America has secured for itself in the economic and political sphere of the world—we must also accept the burdens, practical and moral, of maintaining that place. It is simply bad faith to derive the benefit and then condemn a major source of that benefit.[74]

It seems he would find the position that I am taking to be one of "bad faith." As a U.S. citizen, I appreciate my blessings, opportunities, and freedoms. I have had and still have many. It is possible, even likely, that I don't appreciate them enough. Professor Cook may be right. I may not understand how many of these I have because of our military and its presence.

However, as a citizen of the Kingdom of God with brothers and sisters in 150 countries around the world, I have no interest in seeing America continue to be "the empire." I do not want us to be great and others less. I am quite willing for us to give up that role, even if I lose some civic freedoms. I will respect my government and show respect to all who serve in it, but I will not compromise my allegiance to the Kingdom of God for it. I will not condemn my country for having an army or a police force (for the kingdoms of this world must have such things), but I will not let it become an idol. My role in this world is not to support our military or to be an American patriot. I have a higher allegiance, and my role is to do all that I can to call men and women out of *all* the kingdoms of this world into the Kingdom of God, where they will find real freedom—the freedom to know God, love one another, do "no harm on all his holy mountain" and "learn war no more."

9. What about the two centurions, one in the Gospels and Cornelius in Acts? They are commended for their faith, but not told to leave the military.

I find that for some people this is one of the strongest arguments for allowing Christians to serve in the military. They point out that military service is not mentioned negatively in the New Testament, though there would seem to be numerous opportunities to do so. Special focus is placed on the story of Cornelius in Acts 10 because he was selected to be the first Gentile convert, with no word said about him needing to resign from his occupation. Because of this, I will speak about him, believing everything said regarding him will also apply to the other centurion mentioned in Matthew 8 and Luke 7.

In the case of Cornelius, we have quite a bit of information about his conversion, but no mention of his military occupation being a problem. Augustine used this to reason that Christians could take up arms and go to war.

Before, however, we conclude that this argument from silence is decisive, let's first remember that that type of argument is a shaky one, and second, take a closer look at how this story raises some serious issues.

An argument from silence is dangerous and unreliable. Andy Alexis-Baker goes through various incidents in Jesus' life and shows that with arguments from silence you can have Jesus approving (1) occupying countries and those countries having the right to exploit weaker nations, (2) Roman tax collection that drained resources from an area while giving them to the wealthy elite in Rome, (3) the murder of some Galileans in the midst of their sacrifices, illustrating brutal and repressive measures, (4) kangaroo courts, and (5) even slavery.[75]

Before drawing any conclusion, let's look more closely at the life and role of a centurion. We know that a centurion was expected to have an uncompromising loyalty to Caesar, as he led one hundred men. According to one ancient source the centurion "is to be vigilant, temperate, active and readier to execute the orders he receives than to talk."[76] If ever there was a man who was "not to reason why," but to just do and die, it was a centurion.

We also know enough about orders given to the Roman army, just from Jewish history, to know they maintained control by use of brutal force and harsh methods. Josephus tells us about the behavior of the Roman army in Jerusalem not that many years after the conversion of Cornelius. His account is summarized in these words on the website EyeWitnesstoHistory.com:

> While the Temple was ablaze, the attackers [Roman soldiers] plundered it, and countless people who were caught by them were slaughtered. There was no pity for age and no regard was accorded rank; children and old men, laymen and priests, alike were butchered; every class was pursued and crushed in the grip of war, whether they cried out for mercy or offered resistance.[77]

Such a culture of brutality described here fits with everything we know about the Roman army. Was there anything more antithetical to the Kingdom? Even before his conversion, Cornelius seems to be moving away from this kind of action toward a concern for people (Acts 10:2–4). But it is noteworthy that Peter says nothing as recorded in Scripture about the culture of brutality Cornelius has been in. Yet we know that from his conversion on, it was Jesus who had to be his Lord, not General Vespasian and not Caesar. You can imagine how that would have gone down in Rome. We know that would have brought him into conflict with his superiors. But Luke records nothing about this.

Also, we know a centurion was to provide leadership in the worship of idols. Rome did have a state religion and it included the worship of the emperor's genius. Caesar was both "Lord" and "Savior." The "good news of peace," the *euangellion*, the gospel, was the good news of what the emperor had done to unite the empire and bring about the "Pax Romana," the peace of Rome. But the state religion also required devotion to the empire's deities (various pagan gods, including Jupiter, Juno, Minerva, and Mars, the god of war). Military leaders were to be examples of this devotion and were to serve in an almost priestly role to bring the soldiers to "worship." After the old paganism died out in other parts of Roman society, it still held sway in the army. Luke's account does not mention this change Cornelius would have to a make, but we know it would have been required. *To call Jesus "Lord" was to say that Caesar was not lord.* The fact that Luke does not mention this does not mean it was not required.

Earlier, in answering question 2 in Chapter 8, we mentioned the kind of tasks those in the military were commanded to complete: flogging a fellow soldier when the commander called for disciplinary measures, cutting off the hand of deserters, humiliating defeated peoples, and participating in crucifixions of those deemed to be enemies of the empire. Of course, a centurion would be responsible for making sure these things were done and could himself be executed for shirking a task. The fact that no mention is made of these things does not mean Cornelius could continue these practices (and maybe he had already stopped them).

Acts 10:48 tells that after the baptisms of Cornelius and his household members, Cornelius "asked Peter to stay with them for a few days." Thom Stark notes: "And that is no surprise. If I were a Roman centurion, and if I had just learned that the whole basis for my life's work had been undermined by a Jew—a Jew executed by my own comrades-in-arms, no less!—I would want to hear more about it too."[78]

We would love to know more about the "follow-up" teaching that went on in those extra days, just as we would like to know more about what was included in Peter's "many other words" in Acts 2:40. But given the ethos of the Roman army and the ethos of the Kingdom of God, there surely were many discussions about the clash of values and the decisions that would have to be made. How could Cornelius have remained in his position for very long?

Scripture does not follow his story, so we can't say for certain what he did, but we do know that both the traditions of Roman

Catholic and Eastern Orthodox Churches tell us that Cornelius renounced his allegiance to Caesar and became bishop of Caesarea. According to Orthodox tradition, Cornelius would later be executed in Ephesus for preaching against idolatry. None of this would have been the least bit surprising, given what we know about the Kingdom and the empire. What is instructive about these traditions is not that we can claim that they are as reliable as Scripture, but that they were later passed on in churches that were not believers in pacifism and were not supporting the view that Christians should leave the military.

I personally find the study of Cornelius' conversion in the context of Imperial Rome to be fascinating and filled with nuances that I for a long time missed. This account certainly shows that God's grace can reach even to the most unlikely of places—in this case, the Roman army, and to those in leadership, no less. But one thing this account does not do is establish the validity of military service for disciples. For a decisive word on how to treat our enemies, we must not go to the Cornelius account, but back to Jesus himself. This is where Cornelius would have had to go. He may have done this quickly. He may have done it over time. But if he remained a faithful disciple, he surrendered the whole issue to Jesus.

10
THE TOUGHEST QUESTION

And now we must turn to our last question and to the one that is perhaps the most difficult, at least in my mind, to answer.

10. Isn't it right for Christians to defend the innocent? Doesn't this mean that there will be times when Christians need to use violence to prevent the innocent from being harmed?

Some years ago, I worked with a group of teachers in our fellowship of churches on a number of challenging topics. At one point I submitted a paper to the group that was a much shorter version of what you find in this book. There was a great deal of hardy discussion. After health issues caused me to step down from the group, they made the decision to release two papers to our churches: The first was mine. The second paper was one written in response to mine. For the sake of discussion, I am going to call the author of that paper "Alan," which just happens to be my middle name. Alan offered the approach of "selfless defense of the innocent." I think what he wrote represents the greatest challenge to the thesis of this book. Because I want to be fair, I am going to include Alan's paper in full, and it follows.

A Friend's Paper: Love Your Enemy – the Dilemma

An ethical dilemma arises when one faces an apparent conflict between two moral imperatives. To obey one command would result in transgressing the other. Jesus purposefully orchestrated conflicts (and resolved them) to highlight a new teaching or challenge a worldview. For example, on the Sabbath just before he delivers his sermon on the plain, Jesus asked a man with a withered hand to come forward (Luke 6:6–11). The crowd of biblical experts "fixed their eyes on Jesus to see whether he would heal on the Sabbath" (thereby transgressing their interpretation of the Law). Two moral imperatives were about to clash before their eyes: healing a hurting man or honoring the command to keep the Sabbath. The tension climaxed as Jesus presented the clarity of the dilemma.

> Then Jesus said to them, "I ask you, which is lawful on the Sabbath: to do good or to do harm, to save life or destroy it?"

Jesus chose to do good, to save, to heal the man. But how would he have chosen to do evil, to destroy life? By doing nothing when he had the opportunity to do good—even on a Sabbath.

Soon after this incident, Jesus presents some of his most revolutionary teaching (Luke 6:20–49). A most provocative section commands us to "love your enemies, do good to those who hate you, bless those who curse you, pray for those who persecute you. If someone slaps you on one cheek, turn to them the other also."

Considering this teaching, our subcommittee has wrestled with the potential ethical dilemmas that arise from our citizenship in the kingdom of heaven with its moral imperatives to both love your brother/family/neighbor (e.g., 1 John 3:16) and love your enemy (Matthew 5:44).

> Which is lawful when confronted with an enemy seeking to harm your family: to love your family/brother or love your enemy?

And given the number of disciples who serve in militaries, many of our fellowship must wrestle with the dilemma on a more public level.

> Which is lawful when confronted with an enemy nation seeking to harm your nation: to love your family/brothers or love your enemies?

Jesus' Sermon on the Mount/plain brilliantly stretches us to live beyond the cultural pressures of this present age. He strips away our small-minded self-focused entitlements. No more revenge, no more *lex talionis,* no more "that's not fair," and no more self-defense (Matthew 5:39 plus Rom 12:19-21; 2 Cor 11:20; 1 Thess 5:15). Rather, we are to love, lend to, and pray for our enemies, and so we do on our better days. But does this preclude us from protecting the innocents? Jesus makes self-defense indefensible for us, but what about selfless defense? I've concluded that selfless defense of the innocent is not only defensible, it's morally mandated.

To do nothing when I have the power to protect (1 Cor 13:7) allows an innocent to be harmed or even destroyed. Loving my enemy does not mean that I allow him to harm my innocent wife/child/brother/neighbor. If even my dearest friend were seeking to harm my wife/child/brother/

neighbor, I would deploy all necessary means to stop him (not for revenge or even for justice but for the selfless protection of an innocent). While my friend would thank me for preventing his malice, my enemy may not.

Nonetheless, I choose to do good through selfless action and not by doing nothing. Classic pacifists argue that doing nothing is not really nothing; rather, they assert that they are doing something of immense power—they are praying. Such faith is remarkable. However, even the Pharisees would argue that they were more trusting of God by doing nothing other than praying for the afflicted man on the Sabbath in the introductory dilemma.

When the dilemma to love moves from the private to the public life of a disciple, the question of military service comes into focus (as does police work). Can a disciple square military service with the ethical demands of [the] New Testament? The same principle applies. Selfless defense of the innocents trumps doing nothing in the name of loving one's enemy. There should be no inconsistency between our private and public ethics. If military service always violates kingdom ethics, then it would be strange for the NT to consistently highlight positive military metaphors and positive military personnel, for example:

(Here Alan lists the examples we mentioned earlier and addressed in question number 5, above.)

In addition to these references, we meet soldiers on a path to repentance that runs right into John the Baptist in

Matthew 3 and Luke 3. John came preaching of a new kingdom and thus prepared the people for a radically new way of life to prepare for this new kingdom of God. His charge to "repent, for the kingdom of heaven is near" (Matthew 3:2) is the same message that Jesus preached (Matthew 4:17) as he began his public ministry. Within this context of preparation for the new kingdom, soldiers approach John to gain clarity on what they should do in order to produce fruit that proves their repentance. He charges them to stop their extortion and rather be content with their soldier's wage—no "resign your post" or "put away your sword."

An argument from silence? If so, then John was ignoring the elephant in the Jordan—not his style. While the examples of metaphors and soldiers in the New Testament don't settle any issues, they do keep us from overstating the pacifist's case.

A soldier who repents and is baptized into Christ does not need to resign his post if he is not violating his conscience. If his country is engaged in a selfless defense of innocents, then he may not have occasion for moral conflict. However—and this is important to note—*such righteous military action is extremely rare indeed* (emphasis added). If his country engages in unrighteous military initiatives, then he is forbidden to kill. A professional soldier is expected to use his discretion even on the field of battle. If he is called to violate his conscience then he should seek reassignment or resign.

This is not a theoretical issue. I am in daily fellowship with many Christian soldiers. They are currently on career paths that steer them well clear of direct combat. Their contribution to potentially unrighteous combat is not totally different than mine as I pay taxes to fund the same effort. I have not counseled them to resign their posts. Most have been very effective at helping the kingdom break into their bases, forts, ships, and barracks as they have spread the gospel.

However, if a disciple contemplates military service after baptism, *I strongly counsel against enlistment* (emphasis added) as they will face compromising oaths and desensitizing conditioning; plus, there is no guarantee that he or she will not be assigned to a position that violates the demands of life in the kingdom.

> Which is lawful when confronted with an enemy seeking to harm your family: to love your family/brother or love your enemy? Which is lawful when confronted with an enemy nation seeking to harm your nation: to love your family/brothers or love your enemies?

We've failed once by allowing the world to inform our consciences on these vital concerns. That was also a failure of doing relatively nothing. The world's propagandists shouted loudly about patriotism while the kingdom's preachers spoke sparingly on the implications of loving our enemies.

Many of us [leaders] left our brothers and sisters to discern God's will without the full counsel of God on this matter. Let's not fail again through overreaction. Well-informed spiritual brothers disagree on these questions. These ethical dilemmas sharpen our discernment as we strive to live out His kingdom in a fallen world. Let them also strengthen our unity through cooperation but without compromise on His moral imperatives. [The End]

I believe that my friend Alan (and with his real name, he *is* my friend) does raise the question that is probably the toughest for the pacifist. "How Christian is it to not protect the innocent? Doesn't 'selfless' defense of the innocents trump doing nothing?" Alan's well-written paper was persuasive. It was at least persuasive enough that the teachers' group felt it should be offered as an alternative—an alternative that arguably supports what most people already believe.

A Review of "Selfless Defense of the Innocent"

So, is selfless defense of the innocent with the use of violence the last word? Is it a reasonable objection to the pacifist view I have advocated in this book? Can this question be answered?

Let me make several observations:

First, I can agree with many of Alan's points. In many ways, we are not that far apart.

- He appreciates that the kingdom message is a serious and radical call, and I believe he sincerely wants to hold to that.
- He does not believe in *personal self-defense.* He does not believe, it would seem, in carrying a gun to protect yourself. At this point, he takes Jesus' challenging command seriously, and goes further than many believers will go.
- He agrees that the *righteous* use of force (in wartime) is extremely rare.
- He would counsel any new disciple not to enlist in the military because he sees many of the same problems I have described.

My second observation is that doing nothing is not the only possible pacifist response. Doing nothing may very well be what we will do if we fail to "train ourselves to be godly." Those who go to war are highly trained—highly trained in how to kill or destroy the enemy. Loving one's enemy has to be one of the hardest things we are asked to, and if we are not trained in how to do it, we very likely will do nothing. But killing or doing nothing are not the only options. Rosalee Velloso Ewell argues that Christian pacifism is not passive because it: (1) creatively seeks alternatives to the violence of this world, (2) actively engages the powers of violence, even to the point of death, (3) is courageous enough to act like Esther and to face the earthly powers—to the point of putting one's own life on the line, (4) takes responsibility for not killing the oppressor and for finding another way forward, and (5) presumes that prayer is an essential aspect of the Christian life.[79]

Regarding her last point, how much time and prayer do we give to find creative nonviolent ways to respond to those who want to harm us? This is not to say such things will always "work," but the violent responses don't always "work" either.

Third, we must note that "selfless defense of the innocent" has such a right sound to it. How could anyone argue with this? Actually, we can. When we lay it alongside Jesus' actual teaching, we see something else. I don't want to be snarky or to speak with an edge, but here is what happens when we get down to real life: I hear Alan saying that we should teach "love your enemies, give them something to eat and pray for them," but if they should threaten your wife or family or loved ones or an innocent elderly person in your neighborhood or *anyone else* that you deem innocent, you can take violent action against them. *In fact, Alan says that you have a moral obligation to do whatever you need to do to stop them!* And, furthermore, if they should threaten to harm your country when your country hasn't done anything wrong (in your judgment), you should also take whatever action is needed, including violence, to stop them.

When I think about that, I cannot see that we are ending up with a radical and challenging ethic. This is pretty much what most people already believe. This is hardly the invasion of a whole new way of thinking (which *is* found in the Sermon on the Mount). This is what most soldiers of most countries think they are doing. They see themselves as representing the good guys against the bad guys in defense of the innocent. This is what most people in my country are thinking when they buy and keep loaded guns in their homes. The language in Alan's paper masks the fact that this is an endorsement of what 90% of people believe they are already doing and not a message that says, "What are you doing more than others?" (Matthew 5:47).

Try to imagine a disciple having time in prayer and reading these teachings of Jesus about loving your enemy. Now see him or her the next day shooting the enemy to pieces with an M-16. By participating in war, what he or she does is the same as what others do. Where is the dramatic difference that could send light beaming out into the world?

Fourth, it would seem right to make an assumption if, as Alan writes, we have a moral obligation to defend the innocent: in every country where it is legal to own and bear arms, every disciple should do this because it will greatly increase our ability to defend and protect the innocent. Particularly, in the United States, where innocent people come under fire almost every day (there were 340 mass shootings in 2018), why shouldn't every Christian be armed and ready to protect the innocent? If this is the right direction, then the Sanctuary Church north of Philadelphia was doing well when they encouraged everyone to bring their weapons one Sunday so they could pray over them and bless them. Referring to the school shooting in Florida, the minister of Sanctuary said, "If the football coach who rushed into the building to defend students from the shooter with his own body had been allowed to carry a firearm, many lives, including his own, could have been saved." If we have a high calling to protect the innocent, this pastor would seem to be right. But is this what Jesus would have the church look like? Is this the Jesus and the Kingdom that Isaiah foretold? Is this the Jesus of the Beatitudes? Should his church be an armed camp?

Fifth, I would say that we are making a huge assumption when we argue that the use of violence, particularly killing another person, is the most loving thing we can do for family or other innocent persons. *We don't really know that.* That appears to be right according to human wisdom, but many things humans try have all kinds of unintended consequences. When we say it is okay to suspend Jesus' teaching in certain situations, we may just be taking a big step away from God's wisdom that looks like foolishness to the world.

Sixth, we don't find in the new covenant Scriptures any encouragement for us to defend an innocent life by taking another. We know Jesus was an innocent man, but he forbids his disciples from trying to protect him. If we say that was so that God's redemptive purpose could be accomplished, we have the situation where Stephen was an innocent, but no efforts were made to protect him. I do not know of one story from at least the first 150 years of church history where Christians are said to have struck back to protect the innocents. If protecting the innocents was one of the moral obligations of the early Christians, they apparently did a very poor job of carrying it out. Many of them died for their faith, with tradition telling us that was true of all the apostles except John. *They were willing to die for their faith but not kill for it.*

Seventh, how do we ever know that our country is "the good guy" and the other country is "the bad guy" and that we are defending the innocents? Governments are notorious for hiding many things from their people. As you commit yourself to obey your commanding officers and kill those who they say are the enemies, you have no idea what really may be going on behind the scenes. Governments will do everything they can to convince their people that their cause is just. That is often rightly called propaganda, but many things are kept hidden from view. It is said that one of the reasons the Nazis were successful in keeping the support of the German people is that they so skillfully kept hidden their worst atrocities.

In connection with this, let's suppose two soldiers who are followers of Jesus in separate countries have accepted Alan's view. They at some point may be going to war against each other with each one having believed the narrative of their president, prime minister, or premier. "Kelsey" and "Sasha" could be shooting at each other on the battlefield, both believing they *have a moral imperative to kill the other*. In that moment who is the Lord of their lives and what message is being proclaimed to the world? How is God's will being done on earth as it is in heaven?

My eighth observation has to do with this quote from Alan: "A professional soldier is expected to use his discretion even on the field of battle. If he is called to violate his conscience then he should seek reassignment or resign." Alan is right, but the complex conundrum comes when another element of the military code is considered: *refusal to obey an order is a serious crime,* which, if committed in combat, is punishable by death. On one side, a soldier is in a culture where the chain of command and the need to obey orders is greatly stressed, even held sacred. On the other side, there is the need to be sure the order is lawful, which does not get nearly as much emphasis.

How could it? If soldiers were to question orders on a regular basis, it would severely cripple the ability of an army to fight effectively. In addition, all this puts great pressure on the soldier to evaluate very challenging ethical situations in the midst of trying to follow orders when bullets are flying and bombs exploding. Who can weigh out all that is involved in order to do the right thing in that situation?

Finally, I would ask, when should the soldier seek reassignment or resign? After she follows orders and the result is the death of civilians (innocents)? Or after she disobeys orders and is court-martialed? Why put oneself, as a disciple, in such an ethically ambiguous situation in the first place? Why be in a circumstance where you have been trained to kill? Is that our role now as citizens of heaven?

Admittedly, it is a tough question: "Isn't it right for Christians to defend the innocent? Doesn't this mean that there will be times when Christians need to use violence to stop the innocent from being harmed?" For some, these are easy to answer. For the nonviolent they are a challenge. I believe that Alan offers his view in all good faith, and with the emphasis on "selfless" and "innocents," his words seem to fit with Jesus' message.

Yet, upon closer examination, I find it to be very much like the world's "reasonable" view, and not a revolutionary kingdom view. It opens the door to much subjectivity about who the "innocents" are, particularly in the case of war. It leads to a situation where Christians could be killing one another with all parties believing they are being righteous. Nothing could fly more in the face of the Kingdom. It sounds as if Alan's view gives us *a moral responsibility* to take certain violent action that we never find Jesus encouraging or early Christians taking. Overall, it does not fit with the tenor and nature of the revolutionary Kingdom that Jesus proclaimed. It teaches "Love your enemy except in these circumstances…"

After considering the abundance of teaching from Matthew 5, Luke 6, and Romans 12, we must not let our final posture on these crucial questions be determined by some hypothetical worst-case scenario that has never happened to us or to most people we know. It seems that way of decision-making is motivated far more by fear than by faith or by love.

I have a friend who changed and became a believer in nonviolence. Now he prays that God will keep him from ever being in one of these worst-case scenarios. I don't know what he will do if he finds himself in one of those, but his approach honors the teaching of Jesus and better prepares him, come what may. None of us who embraces a nonviolent posture can be sure what we will do if suddenly endangered or if someone we love is unexpectedly threatened, but I can be quite sure what I will do if I do not seriously train myself to think differently about such experiences (1 Timothy 4:7). This is a far cry from being passive and doing nothing.

Preston Sprinkle writes this about the effect of living the Sermon on the Mount:

> Welcome to Jesus' upside-down kingdom... Heads will turn as we turn our cheeks. Our inexplicable behavior will call attention to our inexplicable God. Light will beam across our dark world as we love the spouses who don't love us back, keep our word when it hurts, judge ourselves rather than others, and—most shockingly—love our enemies who are harming us.[80]

To the extent that we make exceptions to Jesus' message, we give in to our fears and turn down the light or maybe put it out altogether.

11

PRACTICAL PARTICULARS

Having looked at some questions raised by those who challenge the pacifist point of view, I want to turn now, more briefly, and look at some practical issues that might be raised as we put this teaching into practice.

1. *What should a disciple do who is in the military, but comes to a new conviction that he or she cannot and will not kill another human being?* Each situation will be different, but we can give some general guidelines.

   a. First, do not doing anything in haste. Makes sure you have written down your thoughts and spent time in prayer. Read widely about conscientious objection or objectors (COs).

   b. Second, seek out help from the spiritual leaders in your life. If possible, set up time with an elder, or at least a ministry leader, and share your story with them. Let them know why you have come to your new conviction and ask for their thoughts.

   c. Third, find out what your options are according to the military code or the laws for the country you live in. In the U.S. those on active duty can still apply for CO status, but you need to know all the rules. You can find these and other helpful material at these websites: www.

centeronconscience.org and girightshotline.org. Especially useful is the article titled "6 Myths About Conscientious Objection" that you can find at the latter site.

d. Fourth, prepare yourself for a long and possibly unpleasant process. This is not something the military in the U.S. welcomes, and that is something that will likely be true everywhere. One report says that only about 100 such claims are submitted annually in the U.S., but the number is rising. After you apply, you must have interviews with (1) a psychiatrist, (2) a chaplain, and (3) an investigating officer. You will likely feel as if you are on trial. Don't be surprised if questions are raised about your mental health.

d. Finally, and somewhat ironically, make sure you put on the full armor of God described in Ephesians 6. As you decide that it is no longer your role to fight in physical warfare, you will discover the spiritual warfare will grow more intense. Opposition may come from some surprising places. You will need much help from God and from your brothers and sisters, but you will also be given the opportunity to show Jesus in some powerful ways.

2. *How should a disciple with the pacifist conviction feel about those who serve in the military?* "Feel" is probably not the right word. "Treat" is probably the right word and the answer is to love. We should have it and do it toward everyone. If you have decided that you are going to love your enemy and treat them as a neighbor, then most certainly you are going to love your fellow citizen (who may oppose you like an enemy).

You are certainly, also, going to love a fellow disciple who has made a different decision from the one you have made. You have decided that you cannot do some things they still believe they should do, but your role is not to condemn them, give them the cold shoulder, or look for ways to express your disapproval. Your first order of business is not to preach against the military, but to proclaim the Kingdom of God both with your words and your life, with the latter being crucial. I have no better counsel to give than what Peter wrote to the "aliens and strangers" of his day: "But in your hearts revere Christ as Lord. Always be prepared to give an answer to everyone who asks you to give the reason for the hope that you have. But do this with gentleness and respect, keeping a clear conscience, so that those who speak maliciously against your good behavior in Christ may be ashamed of their slander" (1 Peter 3:15–16, emphasis added). One does great harm to the Kingdom if he argues for loving enemies but does not show gentleness and respect to those he reaches out to. If you need to, reread Chapter 1 of this book and remember to appreciate many things about the military and to show proper respect to everyone (1 Peter 2:17).

3. *How should we view those who come back from war badly damaged by it—physically, emotionally, spiritually, and morally?* My guess is that most of you can answer this as well as or better than I can. Again, Peter's words are so right and timely: "Finally, all of you, be like-minded, be sympathetic, love one another, be compassionate and humble" (1 Peter 3:8). Sympathetic, compassionate, humble. We need to care for those who are wounded and hurt. This is no place or time for

judgment and especially for condemnation. One of my joys is to support a favorite nonprofit organization that reaches out to people, including former soldiers, who are seeking to recover from traumatic experiences that have robbed them of hope and joy.

4. *How should disciples of Jesus with enemy-love convictions feel about the honoring of the military in the meetings of the church, for example, on Memorial Day or Veterans Day?*

There is a challenge here for me. Sometimes this is related to a celebration of patriotism in the sense of one nation over another. I cannot endorse that. On the other hand, sometimes it is just the show of appreciation to those who have served and put something bigger than themselves ahead of their own self-interest. That is something I can participate in. I think it is best if the church recognizes that these are essentially national and civil celebrations. However, if we have those in the church who want to recognize the veterans among us, I think there are ways to do that without endorsing war, and all the while, communicating to the church that as followers of Jesus we are to be always working for peace. Whatever we do, we must do it emphasizing that there is a big difference between the empires of this world and the Kingdom of God, and that our loyalty is always ultimately to the latter, and must not be confused with loyalty to the state.

5. *How does all that has been said in this book relate to the work of the police? Specifically, is policework something that Christians can in good conscience engage in?* While I will not try to tackle this issue in full, I think a few things can be said to help us begin a discussion.

a. Scripture recognizes the need for the police function, and that is actually what is being talked about in Romans 13, although in the Roman Empire soldiers often carried out the police role.
b. Those fulfilling the police role are being servants of God (verse 4), and disciples are to be submissive to those serving in that way. In my mind that would involve notifying them when illegal activity occurs that threatens one's neighbors or the peace and security of one's community.
c. As already pointed out in Chapter 9, there is a contrast between the Christian's role and the role of the state. The Christian does not execute vengeance on those who do wrong (Romans 12) but that is the role of the state (Romans 13).
d. Generally, the same arguments used against the disciple being in the military would be used against a disciple serving as a police person. For those who believe that it is not the Christian's role to ever take life or use violence, they could not serve as a police person, for they must be ready to do both. However, there are some writers and teachers who feel there is enough of a difference between the military and the police function as to allow a Christian to serve in the latter. I am not persuaded that this is true.
e. As I finished writing this book, the police in three different world cities had been involved in clashing with peaceful protesters. In all three places the police were instructed to beat protesters. In one situation the police used live bullets and people died. The police were just

following orders. Should a Christian be in that space doing that kind of work?

6. *What do you mean when you say, "Soldiering is not our role?"*
This question doesn't perfectly fit in this chapter, but since I have mentioned this several times and just did again in the question above, let me elaborate.

It is not that soldiering or policing is evil or sinful, the way stealing or lying are sinful. It is just that once we are in the Kingdom, as citizens of heaven, these jobs are not our role. (In the same way, I think a strong case can be made for the fact that being a politician is not our role, although I will not make that case here.) We have been called to do something else in this world, and what we have been called to does not fit well with being a soldier (or police officer or politician). We have been called to something much different—we might rightly say, higher.

David Hicks was in the Army from 1958 to 1978, retiring as a Sergeant Major. Once out, he went to Princeton Theological Seminary, and then returned to the Army as a chaplain.[81] In that process, his role changed, since chaplains do not carry weapons and do not engage in combat. What was entirely appropriate during one phase of his service was completely different once he took on a new role. An internet article documents the exploits of "Twelve Heroic Military Chaplains." Most received awards for their service, often posthumously, but none of those exploits involved taking another life or harming an enemy.[82] These men all understood that they had a different role from their fellow soldiers. In the same way, I would say that once the Prince of Peace has become our commanding officer, we have a new role and a higher loyalty.

12
A "DISPUTABLE" MATTER?

You have stayed with me through four chapters of questions and answers. I hope you can stay with me for one more. The question that some of you, no doubt, have had while reading this book is this: *Why not treat this entire issue as a "disputable matter" or "opinion" and leave it to each Christian to decide for themselves what is right?* After all, as Alan points out in his paper, "Well-informed spiritual brothers disagree on the military issue." For many people that truth is enough. There is no need to seek consensus and maybe no need to bring it up for discussion, because we don't want to highlight our disagreements.

A Romans 14 Issue?

There are those who point to Romans 14 and say, "Why not apply Paul's principal from verse 1 and verse 5?": "Accept the one whose faith is weak, without quarreling over disputable matters.… One person considers one day more sacred than another; another considers every day alike. Each one should be fully convinced in their own mind." We need to look at this more carefully.

Paul identifies some things that are opinion matters: the types of food we eat, what days we designate as holy, whether we drink wine or not. Michael Burns points out that these all had to do with the cultural clashes between those with Jewish and Gentile backgrounds. Whatever their origins, Paul is convinced that these things are really *a matter of indifference* to God (Romans 14:14), but they can affect

Christian fellowship if we ignore one another's convictions. The key word here, as pointed out by Fee and Stuart, is "indifference."[83] These are matters of inconsequence, so we must not divide the body over these things. A so-called "disputable matter" (probably a poor translation) is not just some matter that is disputed. Perhaps we gain insight if we compare three other translations of Romans 14:1:

- "As for the one who is weak in faith, welcome him, but not to quarrel over opinions." ESV
- "Now accept the one who is weak in faith, but not for the purpose of passing judgment on his opinions." NASB
- "Now receive the one who is weak in the faith, and do not have disputes over differing opinions." NET BIBLE

Romans 14 refers to differing opinions on matters that are cultural and *not* of major import. These things are not what the Kingdom of God is about. But the Kingdom of God is about righteousness (read, for example, "Do to others as you would have them do to you"), peace (read, for example, not war, not strife, not retaliation) and joy in the Holy Spirit (Romans 14:17).

While the types of food we eat, whether we drink wine, what days we make special, and a variety of other issues often issuing from different cultures are matters of opinion, some things are so central to the Kingdom of God that we are not at liberty to have different views. (Of course, we may differ, but we must work hard not to leave a matter there.) *The issue of loving our enemies is not a matter of indifference to God.* It is part of the higher righteousness Jesus called us to in the Sermon on the Mount. It does not belong on Paul's list with meat, vegetables, wine, and special days. It is at the heart of how the

Kingdom is so different from the world. Let's listen again to Jesus' words:

> But I tell you, love your enemies and pray for those who persecute you, that you may be children of your Father in heaven. He causes his sun to rise on the evil and the good, and sends rain on the righteous and the unrighteous. (Matthew 5:44–45)

> "But to you who are listening I say: Love your enemies, do good to those who hate you, bless those who curse you, pray for those who mistreat you....
>
> If you love those who love you, what credit is that to you? Even sinners love those who love them. And if you do good to those who are good to you, what credit is that to you? Even sinners do that.... But love your enemies, do good to them, and lend to them without expecting to get anything back. Then your reward will be great, and you will be children of the Most High, because he is kind to the ungrateful and wicked. Be merciful, just as your Father is merciful." (Luke 6:27–36)

Whether we respond to an enemy with love or with a bullet, a bomb, or a bayonet is not a matter of indifference to God. It is not a disputable or opinion matter in the sense that we find in Romans 14. Our only option as disciples is to respond with love (God helping us, of course, to do what is so unnatural). While I can think of a number of times when we might rationalize and defend the use of violence, I cannot think of any words in the New Testament that would encourage us, as disciples, to that action for any reason.

But the truth is, right now in our churches, the disciple and war is a *de facto* "opinion matter" (with the Christian pacifist view being the "odd" opinion). This is not because it is a matter of indifference to God, but just because we have different opinions about it. It is interesting to contrast this with how we view abortion, which, incidentally, is not mentioned in the Scriptures. I am confident that most readers of this book do not view abortion as an opinion matter even though people in the United States and many other countries are sharply divided on it. Those who feel, as I do, that it is not an opinion matter, strongly believe as they do because it involves life and death—life and death of one made in the image of God, which is never a matter of indifference to God.

Does This Question Belong in the "Opinion" Box?

The issue of the Christian and the military is just as important, and whatever we do with it, we must not drop it in the box of "opinion matters/issues of indifference to God." It does not belong there in Paul's Romans 14 box. But that is where we have put it. Surely that cannot be right. The Kingdom of God is *about* vital issues like this. It also is a matter of life and death (as is the Christian view of the death penalty). All of this greatly matters to God, and we must seek his view of it.

The pragmatist looks at our church landscape and says, "We must view it as an opinion matter *because we do in fact* have different opinions about it, and if we can't unite on one view, our only alternative would be to divide the fellowship."

Try to stay with me here. My question: Is that truly our only alternative? My thought is that this type of thinking has allowed us to be lazy and just see the status quo as our only option. So we don't study and we don't pray, and we don't ask God to show us his will on a difficult matter. We decide in advance that we, though we are members of the Kingdom of God, won't ask, won't seek, and won't knock. We will just accept the status quo. We won't even try to find unity. We will not try something that might fail.

If it will not go in the opinion box because it is not an indifferent matter to God, we must believe God can and will lead us to a unified view of what kingdom thinking means on this point, as he already has on some other key points. I am ready to express that faith. I am ready to issue a call for us to be a Kingdom-seeking people who search for God's will on this topic of enemy-love. I also want to ask our leaders to do just that…lead us. We need you. *This is not a matter of indifference to God and we must not leave it in the opinion box. It must not be a matter of indifference to us.*

Septima Clark has been called "the most important woman you never heard of." Martin Luther King called her the architect of the Civil Rights Movement. She once gave five key principles to those who trained with her. One of those was, "Have a bold idea—an idea that is more bold than anyone is comfortable with." That is what I think is needed here.

I am writing this in March 2019. In a period of twenty-two days in February and March, I have seen two of my closest brothers in my congregation (and fellow members of the septuagenarian club) die and go be with Christ, which is far better for them (Philippians 1:23), though it leaves me grieving. Both of them were examples to me in running the race to the absolute finish. Inspired by my two friends, I want to offer a bold idea. I want to call us "to dream the impossible dream" and go on "a glorious quest" seeking to be one in heart and mind with Jesus' kingdom message to love our enemies.

But what if we don't find that unity? On the one hand, let's believe we can. On the other hand, since I am advocating for Jesus' message of astonishing love, I certainly will not stop loving any of you, even if we cannot agree. I am not going to make a judgment about your commitment or spirituality, wherever you land; but I still have to ask you to be a part of this quest—the quest for us to let the kingdom message—the heaven-breaking-into-the-present-age message—be the one that influences how we treat our enemies. Surely, this matters to God. Surely, he will help us find unity. Let's start with some serious conversations.

The Power of Kingdom Moments

October 2, 2006, marked the beginning of what might have been the most unlikely, but the most powerful, series of "religious" events (if we dare to call them that) so far in the twenty-first century. However, you may be surprised at what I will share. On that date a shooting occurred at the West Nickel Mines School, a one-room schoolhouse in an Amish community in Lancaster County, Pennsylvania. Charles Carl Roberts IV, who was himself a husband and father of three, took hostages and shot eight out of ten Amish girls (ages six to thirteen). Five of them eventually died. Roberts committed suicide in the schoolhouse as state and local police surrounded the small building. School shootings are, sadly, not unusual in my country. The response of the Amish community, however, was beyond unusual. What they did was widely discussed in the national media and continues to have impact on people's lives today.

The Amish, who are sometimes called Old Order Mennonites, trace their roots back to the Anabaptist movement in the times of the Reformation, and after 500 years, they have never stopped teaching Jesus' message about loving their enemies, nonviolence, forgiveness, and reconciliation. So, within hours of the murders, a leader of the Amish community came to the home of the parents of Charles Roberts, the murderer, to assure them that they did not see them as

A *"Disputable" Matter?* 177

enemies, but as friends, and knew they were grieving the death of their son.

Ten years later a *Washington Post* article documented how the Amish continued to reach out to the Roberts family, affirming their forgiveness and building a profound life-changing friendship.[84] By embracing the upside-down message of the Kingdom of God, a community of humble folk in rural Pennsylvania got the attention of the world and shined a light into the darkness. I don't think the Amish get everything right, and I fail to see the connection between faith and not using modern conveniences, but we have to recognize and appreciate the powerful effect that is seen when a community of faith *unites* around this countercultural message of Jesus and his Kingdom.

Will you ask, seek, and knock, and encourage all God's people to seek God's will on this matter wherever we are right now? If we ask, we will receive. If we seek, we will find. Can you imagine the impact our unity on "loving our enemies" would have?

13

SUMMING UP

So, what have we seen?

- The long-awaited Kingdom of God came in Jesus.
- In the Kingdom, the age to come was breaking into the present age, while we still await the consummation of the Kingdom in Jesus' Second Coming.
- Jesus' revolutionary kingdom message turned most everything upside down.
- He said, "You've heard it said… But I say to you…" (and then came the new kingdom perspective).
- He taught the revolutionary idea of loving your enemies and doing good to those who would harm you.
- Jesus fulfilled all the words of Isaiah about God's kingdom of peace and he came as the Prince of Peace.
- He rebuked his leading disciple for holding on to the world's wisdom instead of trusting in God's wisdom.
- He transformed a militant zealot into an enemy-loving proclaimer of this peaceable Kingdom.
- Jesus proclaimed that his Kingdom was not of this world. Therefore, his followers would not fight with worldly weapons to advance it, and they never did.

Summing Up

- He lived out God's foolish wisdom by going to the cross and laying down his life, thereby setting the example for all those who would follow him.

- The reality, truthfulness, and power of his kingdom message were proven true when God raised him from the dead, never to die again.

- After Peter was rebuked for using his sword, never in the Scriptures do we see a disciple of Jesus use a weapon to harm another person.

- After Jesus, other writers of Scripture continue to call us to practice nonviolence and do good to all men.

- For almost 300 years, every Christian writer would speak against training for war and against disciples using violence.

- Leaders understood that soldiering was not the Christian's role. Disciples were called to another mission.

- Christians would die for their faith, but they would not kill for it.

- Today, however, about 1800 years later, we do not enjoy the same unity in this matter that the church did for three centuries.

- We have moved a vital matter to the margins and made it a matter of personal opinion, but those who focus on kingdom teaching usually come to a different conclusion.

- Most do not love war, but still believe that, for disciples, the military is honorable service, even when it calls for harming and killing enemies. They believe that the end often justifies the means.

- To be a part of the military involves turning some of the most significant moral issues of life over to someone else who will define for you who is the enemy and what you must do to the enemy.

- Most disciples do not search, study, or investigate this matter, but simply go along with the culture. Though it may have never occurred to them what they are doing, they treat this matter as a "Romans 14 issue," one that is of indifference to God.

- But it should not be this way and it does not have to be this way.

- If we decide to ask, seek, and knock, our Father will not give us a stone. Those who hunger and thirst for righteousness will be filled.

- There will be some challenges and bumps in the road, but the Father will help us unite around the kingdom way to think, and together our light can shine in the darkness.

※

All of us face a decision. But it is not first a decision to be in the military or not. It is not first a decision about using force or not. It is this decision: Will we ask, seek, and knock? Will we hunger to know God's will? Will we pray, "Your Kingdom come"? Will we let the decisions we make be based on the character and the spirit of the Kingdom of God?

14
MIND CHANGE AND... "BUT, GOD"

Before we conclude, I want to give you what may be the most surprising and unusual chapter you will find in a book like this. It is not one that I expected to write. It may especially seem a quite odd way to end our discussion. One early reader felt I should take it out altogether. You may agree with him. But I am leaving this because I was moved to stray from the normal academic playbook and be honest about how I wrestled with this topic and this book.

If am to judge from the feedback I have received from readers, one book I have written has had more impact than any other: *Mind Change: A Biblical Approach to Overcoming Life's Challenges.* My first full-length book, it is maybe the most practical of my writings. Without question, it is the one that most puts my own weaknesses on full display. Let me connect that first book from twenty-five years ago with this latest one you are reading now.

This has not been an easy book to write. I have had many internal battles and temptations to turn back. There have been many times when I have had to engage in the kind of "mind change" I first wrote about two and a half decades ago. If you are familiar with that earlier book, you will recognize the process:

"My thoughts say" and here I describe the doubts, the fears, the negative tapes that run in my mind, like "This is too hard. MS is a nasty, brutal disease. Emotionally, I feel whipped. I'm not sure I am the one who can do this. How could a Christian feel this depressed?"

"'But God' thinking says," and here I refuse to let the negative tapes have the last word, but respond with something like: "Yes, all that may seem true, but God has promised to provide power you don't have and to even use you in your weakness. He often takes people who are a mess and raises them up for his purposes."

In writing this book, here are some of the ways I had to apply what I learned all those years ago dealing with my life with MS, depression, and anxiety. (And, by the way, I need those lessons now as much as I did then.)

> *My thoughts say:* "You know the message of non-resistance and enemy-love is totally impractical. It just does not face the facts of the real world."
>
> *"But God" thinking says:* "If Jesus isn't true and real, that is exactly right, but Jesus is true and the reality behind the universe."

> *My thoughts say,* "Are you sure you want to write about something so controversial?"
>
> *"But God" thinking says:* "Don't ever write to be controversial, but do write, if it's a crucial teaching of Jesus…even if it is controversial."

> *My thoughts say:* "Non-resistance is far too radical. Why not go out being known as the author of nice books on overcoming and having humility? Why advocate such a fringe position?"
>
> *"But God" thinking says:* "Take no thought about your legacy. The words of Jesus are like a fire that you must not hold in." (Thank you, Jeremiah).

My thoughts say: "What you are saying disagrees with what most Christians have said for about 1800 years. Do you think you know more than all those people?"

"But God" thinking says: "All that really matters is what Jesus taught and what message fits with his teachings about the Kingdom of God. The church in the second and third centuries, right after Jesus, taught this, but even if they had not, your call is to be faithful to Jesus as Lord."

My thoughts say: "Tom, you are seventy-two years old, you have multiple sclerosis, your wife has serious health challenges; so why plunge into something that may be exhausting? Why not just stay as comfortable as you can? Why take on something so emotional?" (Do I ever hear this voice!)

"But God" thinking says: "You decided a long time ago to go the way of the cross, not the highway of ease. Are you giving up on that message? And isn't God's love greater than all your fears?"

My thoughts say: "Tom, yes, you feel passionately about this issue. You want to pass on your conviction, especially to those who are younger, but you have lost your touch, man, and if you do a bad job with this book or overlook something important or have faulty logic, you may do more harm than good. It may be a long time before some people will even consider the matter again."

"But God" thinking says: "Everything you have ever written has been written out of your weakness, not out of your strength. Why should this be any different? Yes, you

are older. You think slower. You type slower and make more errors. But didn't God say that he did not take delight in the strength of a horse or the legs of a man, but that he delights in those who fear him and put their hope in his unfailing love?"

My thoughts say: "Tom, the church doesn't want to hear this. It is an inconvenient truth. It is too much of a sticky wicket. It will get no traction. Leaders will avoid it like a political third rail."

"But God" thinking says: "Didn't God tell Jeremiah to speak anyway? Your writing must not be based on polling or popularity. What matters is proclaiming the Kingdom. (And, then, too, you might need to have more confidence in your brothers and sisters.)"

My thoughts say: "There will be those who disagree with you here and, for them, this will sully the whole Kingdom series and everything you wanted to focus on regarding it."

"But God" thinking says: "Your focus must be on proclaiming 'the whole will of God,' and let the chips fall where they may."

So, through a lot of mental and spiritual battles, you have this book because again and again, there was a mind change; and it seems to me that "But God" thinking won the day.

I have had the convictions expressed in these chapters since my earliest days as a disciple of Jesus. As an ROTC student (U.S. Army training in university, for you non-U.S. readers), I decided I could not take my WW2, M-1 rifle we were training with, or the M15

I would have been issued later, and shoot and kill another person. Through the years my thoughts have been sharpened and deepened, yet I have had to struggle with the idea of laying them out in this book. You could tell from Volumes One and Two in this series that I held to these principles, but I have felt the need to be more direct. I just want to be real about the struggle involved in getting here.

I am sure I am not the only one who has to wrestle with what to do, say, or teach about enemy-love. This may be Jesus' most challenging teaching. I feel fairly sure that my words in this book have likely set up some struggle within you. So let me ask: How might the "But God" thinking work in your life? Could I speculate? Could it possibly be something like this?

> *Your thoughts may say:* "I don't know why I should even think about this. I am not in the military and don't intend to be. I don't know anybody who is, but this just hurts my brain."
>
> *Doesn't "But God" thinking say:* "But, as a disciple, you are to be telling the world about the good news of the Kingdom, and if this is part of that message, don't you need to have some convictions about it?"

> *Your thoughts may say:* "But this upsets me. I know brothers and sisters who are great disciples and are in the military. How could I take your position and hurt them?"
>
> *Doesn't "But God" thinking say:* "But that is never the way you decide how to live. It's all about what Jesus taught, not about any of the ways others have chosen to follow him. And at the end of the day you are going to treat everyone with respect."

Your thoughts may say: "My dad, my sister, or my aunt was devoted to the military, served sacrificially, and built such great bonds there. How could I ever disrespect what they value and what they have done?"

Doesn't "But God" thinking say: "You did not make your decision about your spiritual life based on the devotion of your family to something different. There are ways to keep Jesus being Lord in your life and still show respect to others (maybe just not the way they want you to)."

Your thoughts may say: "If I agree that this is the way of Jesus and the way of the cross, it will complicate my life. I am one of those people who has made the military my career. I may never be commanded to go into combat. I may never be asked to kill the enemy. I don't have another career plan, and this just doesn't work for me."

Doesn't "But God" thinking say: "You are right in saying it will complicate your life. You will have to have some tough conversations, and maybe make some tough decisions. You will likely make some people very unhappy. You may even suffer. But what does it mean to say: 'I am crucified with Christ. I no longer live, but Christ lives in me'? And didn't Jesus say, 'Teach others to obey all that I have commanded you, and I will be with you to the end of this age?' And won't he do that?"

Your thoughts may say: "But the church will never be united on this matter! It's hopeless."

But, just maybe, "But God" thinking says: "Your job is not to predict. You are not that kind of prophet. Your job is just to seek, trust, and obey."

I can only guess at what your mind and your natural self are saying to you. I can only guess what you will most struggle with. I can only guess how "But God…" thinking needs to work for you. However, if you need to, I would urge you to go through the whole process. Get it all out in prayer. Maybe it will sound something like this:

"Oh, God, this is a big-time problem for me. Jesus taught us to love our enemies and do good to them, but does that mean we who are disciples should not defend our countries? Does that mean that Christians should not train for war and take up weapons? Does that mean we cannot kill those who want to kill us?

"Dear Father, it seems changing my convictions could hurt many others. It seems I could come across as very judgmental. And then, too, I could probably suffer some rejection and some criticism, and I'm not sure I want that.

"Lord, this whole topic makes me anxious. Do I have to deal with it now? Really?

"But my Father, you have blessed me in so many ways and helped me through so many things, and I know you will help me with this. I have fears, but I also have faith. Help my faith to overcome my fears. Help love to overcome my fear. I trust you. You are my God, and my times are in your hands."

In the end, of course, I don't know what your prayer will be or should be. But whatever it sounds like, this I know: God will bless your surrender to him. He will work in the lives of all who say from the heart, "Your kingdom come; your will be done, in our lives on earth, as it is in heaven."

Join me and continue the discussion at <u>tomcast.online</u>.

APPENDIX
KINGDOM LOVE FOR ENEMIES

The material in this appendix is actually a condensed version of Chapter 17 from Volume Two in this series on the Kingdom of God, which deals with Jesus' kingdom teaching in what we call the Sermon on the Mount. The thesis of this book is based on what we wrote early in this chapter. It is placed here for those who might not have ready access to that volume.

> "You have heard that it was said, 'Love your neighbor and hate your enemy.' But I tell you, love your enemies and pray for those who persecute you, that you may be children of your Father in heaven. He causes his sun to rise on the evil and the good, and sends rain on the righteous and the unrighteous. If you love those who love you, what reward will you get? Are not even the tax collectors doing that? And if you greet only your brothers, what are you doing more than others? Do not even pagans do that? Be perfect, therefore, as your heavenly Father is perfect." (Matthew 5:43–48)

For the first time in the Sermon on the Mount (and in the New Testament as it is now arranged) we hear Jesus speak the word "love." How interesting that his first command for us to love found in the Gospels is the command to love our enemies. What the people had heard was "love your neighbor and hate your enemy." This statement was never made in the Old Testament, but one can understand why it would have become a common thought. For one thing, David is found expressing hatred for his enemies often in the Psalms.

Jesus raises the bar as high as it will go in preaching this radical ethic of love: "Love your enemies." Don't hate them; don't be bitter toward them; don't seek revenge; don't hope they will have bad fortune; and don't want to remove them from your sight. No, instead care about them, want them to be blessed, and take action to show goodwill toward them. If we have not realized it already, we certainly see in this command the need for supernatural help to live the kingdom life.

Clear Teaching

In order to consider all the aspects of this teaching it is helpful to look at the parallel verses in Luke 6:27–28, 31, and 35, and also at Paul's words in Romans 12:17–21. When the three texts are examined, we find at least sixteen clear commands:

1. Love your enemies.
2. Pray for those who persecute you.
3. Don't love just your brothers. *To do that is to be like everybody else.*
4. To love like this is to love like God.
5. Have an indiscriminate or perfect love like God has.
6. Do good to those who hate you.
7. Bless those who curse you.
8. Pray for those who mistreat you.
9. Do to your enemies as you would want them to do to you.
10. Do good to your enemies.
11. Lend to them without expecting to get anything back.
12. Do not repay anyone evil for evil.
13. Do not take revenge.
14. If your enemy is hungry, feed him.

15. If your enemy is thirsty, give him something to drink.
16. Do not be overcome by evil, but overcome evil with good.

This is an impressive list, and we must conclude that Jesus' teaching on the subject, which was passed on to Paul, is in no way vague or unclear. The kingdom person is not commanded to feel great affection for their enemy, but is commanded to treat their enemy with concern and goodwill and to do so in very specific ways.

Without a doubt these words of Jesus stir up our thinking. Some of us have been disciples of his for a long time and have never really come to grips with these matters. It is time that we did so.

Raising the Bar

Throughout Matthew 5, at point after point Jesus begins with the common understanding of what would be the right thing to do, and then he raises the bar higher and higher. And if we have followed the trajectory pattern of his points, we are not surprised to see how he calls us to treat our enemy. (See the diagrams in *The Kingdom of God,* Volume Two, Chapter 17.)

Dietrich Bonhoeffer considers that in this passage we find kingdom love truly defined:

> [The disciple's] behavior must be determined not by the way others treat him, but by the treatment he himself receives from Jesus; it has only one source, and that is the will of Jesus. By our enemies Jesus means those that are quite intractable and utterly unresponsive to our love, who forgive us nothing when we forgive them all, who respond to our love with hatred and to our service with derision.... Love asks nothing in return, but seeks those who need it. And who needs

our love more than those who are consumed with hatred and are utterly devoid of love? Who, in other words, deserves our love more than our enemy? Where is love more glorified than where she dwells in the midst of her enemies?[85]

What Are You 'Doing More'?

Having said this, Bonhoeffer then carefully analyzes what he considers to be the most important verse in the passage: verse 47. His point can best be seen by looking at the English Standard Version: "And if you greet only your brothers, *what more* are you doing than others? Do not even the Gentiles *do the same*?" (emphasis added).

He calls attention to the phrase "what more are you doing than others?" "Doing more" translates the Greek word *perrison*, which refers to that which is extraordinary. He contrasts this with the expression "do the same" (to *auto* in Greek), and then he writes:

> What makes the Christian different from other men is the "peculiar," the *perrison*, the "extraordinary," the "unusual," that which is not "a matter of course." This is the quality whereby the better righteousness exceeds the righteousness of the scribes and Pharisees. It is "the more," the "beyond all that." The natural is the *to auto* (one and the same) for heathen and Christian. The distinctive quality of the Christian life begins with the perrison.... The *perrison* never merges into the to auto.... For [Jesus] the hallmark of the Christian is the "extraordinary." The Christian cannot live at the world level, because he must always remember the *perrison*.[86]

Bonhoeffer's emphasis on the word *perrison* seems entirely appropriate, as it is a word that plays a prominent role in the New

Testament. Earlier when Jesus said, "For I tell you that unless your righteousness surpasses that of the Pharisees and the teachers of the law, you will certainly not enter the kingdom of heaven" (Matthew 5:20), he uses a form of the same word.

Consider some other meanings that are associated with this word: more, greater, excessive, abundant, exceedingly, beyond what is anticipated, exceeding expectation; more abundant, going past the expected limit, more than enough. *Perrison* is used in other vital places in the New Testament to refer to the way God relates to us, as in these two examples:

> "The thief comes only to steal and kill and destroy; I came that they may have life, and *have it abundantly.*" (John 10:10 NASB, emphasis added)

> In him we have redemption through his blood, the forgiveness of sins, in accordance with the riches of God's grace that he *lavished* on us with all wisdom and understanding. (Ephesians 1:7–8, emphasis added)

And then, the word is used to describe the off-the-charts spirit of giving found in the disciples in Macedonia in Paul's Second Letter to the Corinthians:

> And now, brothers and sisters, we want you to know about the grace that God has given the Macedonian churches. In the midst of a very severe trial, their overflowing joy and their extreme poverty *welled up* in rich generosity. For I testify that they gave as much as they were able, and even beyond their ability. Entirely on their own. (2 Corinthians 8:1–3, emphasis added)

In the Kingdom, Jesus calls us to the extraordinary, and he believes that because of the "much more of the Heavenly Father," which he describes in Matthew 7, that we can live the "beyond all that." To fail to love our enemies and only love our brothers is to "do the same" that the heathen do. We need to trust that we can live by the power of the age to come and that doing the extraordinary, the amazing, is quite expected.

Today all of us need to be thankful for this truth and this teaching because without it we would not be in the Kingdom of God. Paul reminds us in Romans 5:10, "For if, while we were God's enemies, we were reconciled to him through the death of his Son, how much more, having been reconciled, shall we be saved through his life!" To love our enemies is for us to do with others what God has done with us.

It is interesting to us that people will sometimes hear this teaching and ask, "Who is my enemy?" somewhat reminiscent of the man who asked Jesus, "Who is my neighbor?" It is almost as if they are thinking, "If someone is not my enemy, maybe I don't have to love him." But Jesus' message assumes that we will love our brothers and our neighbors and all those on the continuum even all the way out to our enemies.

In Jesus' kingdom we will love all across the board. So there's no need to ask "Who is my neighbor?" or "Who is my enemy?" If they exist, we are to love them. This includes those who insult you, those who sue you, those who bully you, those who belong to a foreign force that occupies your country, those who defraud you, those who hate your country and want to destroy it, and those who want to blow you up, just to mention a few.

Bonhoeffer goes on to say:

> Christian love draws no distinction between one enemy and another, except that the more bitter the enemy's hatred, the greater his need of love. Be his enemy political or religious, he has nothing to expect from a follower of Jesus but unqualified love. In such love there is no inner discord between private person and official capacity. In both, we are disciples of Christ, or we are not Christians at all.[87]

Public Life and Private Life?

The last part of the quote above is a repudiation of the classic argument formulated first by Augustine and then given great emphasis by Luther. It says that a Christian has a private life and a public life, and that these teachings of Jesus only apply to the conduct of the private life. In other words, when acting in some governmental role, Luther would say the Christian is not bound by this law of love. In such a case he is free to take off his citizenship in heaven and put on his citizenship in his country or his empire.

This position is the one held today by the great majority of people who describe themselves as Christians. It was a position unheard of in the first 250 years of the church's life, but in the post-Constantinian era it has become dominant. Which one do you find more consistent with the teachings of Jesus?

Should a disciple act as a disciple all the time, or are we allowed to act in some other way if in a "public" role? Should we do good to our enemy in our "private" life, but even see a responsibility to harm our enemy in situations in our "public" life? If we as disciples live under the reign of God, are there times when we can legitimately say, "Jesus' words just do not apply to me in these circumstances"? In such a situation are we showing a higher allegiance to someone or something else than we are to Jesus?

John Howard Yoder offered a carefully balanced but compelling insight:

> Christians love their enemies not because they think the enemies are wonderful people, nor because they believe that love is sure to conquer these enemies. They do not love their enemies because they fail to respect their native land or its rulers; nor because they are unconcerned for the safety of their neighbors; nor because another political or economic system may be favored. The Christian loves his or her enemies because God does, and God commands his followers to do so; that is the only reason, and that is enough.[88]

These comments seem most helpful particularly in situations where love for enemies can easily be misunderstood. In the same spirit, we could add that Christians do not love their enemies because they are unconcerned about the welfare of their family or because they do not recognize that some have resisted enemies with a spirit of selfless sacrifice. They love their enemies for the simple reason that this is what Jesus said people living the kingdom life will do.

Be Perfect?

It comes as no surprise, then, that this section ends with this verse: "Be perfect, therefore, as your heavenly Father is perfect" (v48). The call of the Kingdom is to imitate Jesus' love, and he was living out what he learned from the Father. It is a high standard, but it is what Jesus calls us to. We should not understand "be perfect" as meaning without flaws or errors. Jesus is not demanding some kind of sinless perfection. He knows us all too well for that.

The word for "perfect" is *teleios*, which refers to completeness or maturity. But the meaning of Jesus' teaching is found more in the context. Both in Matthew 5:45 and in the parallel in Luke 6:35, it is clear that we are to be like God in the way he is indiscriminate. We are to show as much love to our enemy as to our friend and as much love to the bad person as to the good one. The seriousness of our discipleship is revealed by how wholeheartedly we embrace Jesus' high call, which would seem to reach its pinnacle with this command.

END NOTES

1. In his book, *Nevertheless: The Varieties of Religious Pacifism,* John Howard Yoder says he can identify at least twenty-six types of pacifism, while finding that none of those are centrally based on trying to live as the community of Jesus the Messiah in this present age. For Yoder it is only the latter that we should be interested in as disciples.

2. "Chargers to Host 28th Annual Salute to the Military," *Chargers.com,* Aug 30, 2016, https://www.chargers.com/news/chargers-to-host-28th-annual-salute-to-the-military-at-chargers-49ers-gam-136206.

3. John D. Roth, *Choosing Against War: A Love Greater than Our Fears* (Intercourse, Penn., 2002) 100.

4. Gordon Livingston, "Why should we support the troops?" *Psychology Today,* https://www.psychologytoday.com/us/blog/lifelines/ 201203/why-should-we-support-the-troops (September 9, 2018).

5. "What does the Bible say about a Christian serving in the military?" *Got Questions* https://www.gotquestions.org/military-Christian.html (November 3, 2018).

6. "Des Browne," *Brainy Quote,* https://www.brainyquote.com/quotes/des_browne_712528 (August 15, 2018).

7. Noemie Emery, "What Is Courage?" *Washington Examiner* https://www.washingtonexaminer.com/what-is-courage, December 30, 2014.

8. MarkLeeGreenblatt.com. http://markleegreenblatt.com/news-reviews/articles/.

9. Mark Lee Greenblatt, "What I Learned about Courage from Interviewing our Troops" *Military.com* https://www.military.com/off-duty/books/2015/11/23/three-things-i-learned-about-courage-from-interviewing-our-troop.html (November 3, 2018).

10. Paul Szoldra, "Award-Winning Journalist Perfectly Captures the Reason Soldiers Often Miss Combat," *Business Insider* (September 4, 2018).

11. Ed Anton, Repentance: *A Cosmic Shift of Heart and Mind* (Spring, Texas: Illumination Publishers, 2014).

12. Roth, *Choosing Against War,* 35.

13. Roth, 156.

14. John Howard Yoder, *The Politics of Jesus* (Grand Rapids: Wm. B. Eerdmans, 1993), 51.

15. For years I have found this whole paradigm so crucial that I make it a part of my studies with all those I am trying to help become disciples. You can see how I present this material in a personal study in the Bible studies section of *The Disciple's Handbook,* now published by Illuminations Publishers (ipibooks.com).

16. We must add that archaeologists have not been able to confirm this large number of deaths. Skeletal remains have been found, but not in numbers that can verify Josephus' account.

17. Compare 1 Corinthians 6:9–11.

18. *Didache,* I, 2–3.

19. David Bercot, editor, *A Dictionary of Early Christian Beliefs* (Peabody, Mass.: Hendrickson Publishing, 1998), 677. Unless otherwise noted, all quotes from the early Christian writers will be from this volume, which quotes from the *Anti-Nicene Fathers,* also published by Hendrickson Publishing.

20. Bercot, *A Dictionary of Early Christian Beliefs,* 676.

21. Bercot, 676.

22. Eberhard Arnold, editor, *The Early Christians in Their Own Words* (Walden, NY: Plough Publishing, 1997), 90.

23. Preston Sprinkle, *Fight: A Christian Case for Nonviolence* (Colorado Springs, Colorado: David C. Cook, 2016), Kindle Location 3143–3165.

24. Bercot, *A Dictionary of Early Christian Beliefs,* 680.

25. Testamonia, iii, 106.

26. Bercot, *A Dictionary of Early Christian Beliefs,* 677.

27. Bercot, 677.

28. Tertullian, *De idololatria* (Anti-Nicene Fathers 3:73).

29. Bercot, *A Dictionary of Early Christian Beliefs,* 678.

30. Bercot, 678.

31. Bercot, 678.

32. Bercot, 678.

33. Bercot, 679.

34. Bercot, 678.

35. Bercot, 681.

36. *Epitome of the Divine Institutes,* Chapter 61, http://www.newadvent.org/fathers/0702.htm.

37. Roland H. Bainton, *Christian Attitudes toward War and Peace* (New York: Abington, 1960), 66.

38. Some evidence for similar deliberations has been found in Egyptian writings some centuries before the Greek works. Often overlooked is the fact that Chinese philosophers in the Taoist and Confusion tradition also engaged in similar discussions in ways that paralleled the Western thinkers. However, these played no role in Christian thinking.

39. Augustine, *Letter 138,* Chapter 2, paragraph 14. http://www.newadvent.org/fathers/1102138.htm.

40. At the same time, former U.S. President Jimmy Carter was writing to show that a preemptive attack did not, for other reasons, meet the requirements of the just war doctrine.

41. Roth, *Choosing Against War,* 48.

42. Stephen Evans, "How Soldiers Deal with the Job of Killing," *BBC News,* 11 June 2011, https://www.bbc.com/news/world-13687796.

43. Clete Goetz, "The Personal Nature of Killing," *Company Command,* https://juniorofficer.army.mil/pubs/armymagazine/docs/2005/CC_09-05-killer-instinct.pdf (accessed November 10, 2018).

44. Dave Ross, "Soldiers of Conscience: Interview with Pete Kilner," POV, http://archive.pov.org/soldiersofconscience/interview-pete-kilner/ (Accessed November 11, 2018).

45. Christopher J. Lamb, "Leadership and Operational Art in World War II: The Case for General Lesley J. McNair," *National Defense University Press,* https://ndupress.ndu.edu/Publications/Article/1038851/leadership-and-operational-art-in-world-war-ii-the-case-for-general-lesley-j- mc/.

46. "The Veneer of Civilization: Episode 7," *The Vietnam War,* PBS, 2018.

47. "Moral Injury in the Context of War," *US Department of Veterans Affairs,* https://www.ptsd.va.gov/professional/treat/cooccurring/moral_injury.asp.

48. Peter Kilner, "Moral Injury," *Thoughts of a Soldier-Ethicist,*

http://soldier-ethicist.blogspot.com/2017/03/a-third-form-of-moral-injury.html

49. "The Wounds of a Drone Warrior," *New York Times Magazine,* https://www.nytimes.com/2018/06/13/magazine/veterans-ptsd-drone-warrior-wounds.html (accessed December 14, 2018).

50. "Patterns in conflict: Civilians are now the target," *UNICEF,* https://static.unicef.org/graca/patterns.htm (accessed February 4, 2019).

51. "The Wounds of a Drone Warrior".

52. Chelsea Cook, "Soldier's Suicide Note Goes Viral," CNN, July 6, 2013, https://www.cnn.com/2013/07/06/us/soldier-suicide-note/index.html.

53. "These Are Just Children," CNN, February 27, 2019, https://www.cnn.com/2018/08/13/middleeast/yemen-children-school-bus-strike-intl/index.html.

54. "The Wounds of a Drone Warrior".

55. "Military Veterans Respond to Our Cover Story About Moral Injury" *New York Times,* June 21, 2018, https://www.nytimes.com/2018/06/21/magazine/moral-injury-readers-respond.html.

56. Paul Waldman, "Some Context for Our Upcoming Bombing Campaign," *American Prospect,* August 29, 2013, https://prospect.org/article/some-context-our-upcoming-bombing-campaign.

57. "Gallup: US Population Highly Militaristic," *World Beyond War.org,* https://worldbeyondwar.org/gallup-u-s-population-highly-militaristic/

58. Stanley Hauerwas, "Foreword," *A Faith Not Worth Fighting For: Addressing Commonly Asked Questions about Christian Nonviolence* (Eugene, Oregon: Cascade Books, an Imprint of Wipf and Stock Publishers, 2012), Kindle edition, Kindle location 60.

59. Roth, *Choosing Against War,* 116.

60. "Were the Crusades Just Wars?" *Catholic Answers,* https://www.catholic.com/magazine/online-edition/were-the-crusades-just-wars (accessed September 30, 2018).

61. In his two-volume work, *The Crucifixion of the Warrior God,* Greg Boyd argues that all of the violence attributed to God in the Old Testament must be read through the lens of Christ crucified, which causes us to see something different from what is seen on the surface. That discussion is beyond the scope of this book, but Boyd makes an intriguing but controversial argument you might want to consider.

62. Josephus, *Jewish Wars,* 5.451.

63. Samuel Wells, "Didn't Jesus Say He Came Not to Bring Peace, but a Sword?" *A Faith Not Worth Fighting For,* Kindle edition,162.

64. Also remember Simeon's words to Mary and Joseph in the temple: "And a sword will pierce your own soul too" (Luke 2:35).

65. John Dear, "Didn't Jesus Overturn Tables and Chase People Out of the Temple with a Whip?" *A Faith Not Worth Fighting For,* Kindle edition, 189.

66. For a fuller discussion of Revelation 19 see Nelson Kraybill, "What about the Warrior Jesus in Revelation 19?" *A Faith Not Worth Fighting For,* Kindle edition, 194.

67. Justin Bronson Barringer, "What about Those Men and Women Who Gave Up Their Lives so that You and I Could Be Free?" *A Faith Not Worth Fighting For,* Kindle edition, 95.

68. Martin Luther, *Commentary on the Sermon on the Mount* (Philadelphia: The Lutheran Publication Society, 1892), 196.

69. For a more thorough refutation of this dualism, I would refer readers to Lee Camp's essay "What About Romans 13?" *A Faith Not Worth Fighting For,* Kindle edition,144.

70. Stephen R. Haynes, *The Battle for Bonhoeffer* (Grand Rapids, Michigan: Wm. H Eerdmans, 2018).

71. Barringer, "What About Those Men and Women," 95.

72. Barringer, 95.

73. Barringer, 98.

74. Martin L. Cook, "Soldering: Can a Christian Serve in the Military?" *Christian Century,* July 4, 2001 https://www.christiancentury.org/article//soldiering.

75. Andy Alexis-Baker, "What about the Centurion? A Roman Soldier's Faith and Christian Pacifism," *A Faith Not Worth Fighting For,* Kindle edition, 178.

76. Vegetius, *De Re Militari.*

77. "The Romans Destroy the Temple at Jerusalem, 70 AD," *Eye Witness to History,* http://www.eyewitnesstohistory.com/jewishtemple.htm (accessed May 6, 2019).

78. This quote comes from research I did several years ago. Numerous attempts to find and document the source on the internet proved unsuccessful. It appears the website has been taken down.

79. C. Rosalee Velloso Ewell, "Isn't Pacifism Passive?" *A Faith Not Worth Fighting,* Kindle Edition, 12–17.

80. Preston Sprinkle, Fight: *A Christian Case for Nonviolence,* Kindle Locations 2102–2105.

81. Erik Slavin, "Army Career Comes Full Circle as Chaplain Returns to DMZ," *Stars and Stripes,* May 27, 2007, https://www.stripes.com/news/army-career-comes-full-circle-as-chaplain-returns-to-dmz-1.64589.

82. Miss Cellenia, "Twelve Heroic Military Chaplains," *Mental Floss,* January 10, 2012, http://mentalfloss.com/article/29695/12-heroic-us-military-chaplains.

83. Gordon D. Fee and Douglas Stuart, *How to Read the Bible for All Its Worth* (Zondervan, 1981, 1993, 2003), Kindle location, 1375.

84. Colby Itkowitz, "Her son shot their daughters 10 years ago. Then, these Amish families embraced her as a friend," *Washington Post,* October 1, 2016, https://www.washingtonpost.com/news/inspired-life/wp/2016/10/01/10-years-ago-her-son-killed-amish-children-their-families-immediately-accepted-her-into-their-lives/?utm_term=.ab56ed3f3cbc.

85. Dietrich Bonhoeffer, *The Cost of Discipleship* (New York: Simon and Shuster, 1937, 1959, 1975), 146.

86. Bonhoeffer, 152.

87. Bonhoeffer, 146.

88. John Howard Yoder, "Living the Disarmed Life," *A Matter of Faith, Sojourners' Magazine Study Guide* (January 1982).

BIBLIOGRAPHY

Bonhoeffer, Dietrich. *The Cost of Discipleship,* New York: Simon and Schuster, 1937, 1959, 1975.

Bercot, David. *The Kingdom that Turned the World Upside Down,* Amberson, Pennsylvania: Scroll Publishing, 2003.

Burns, Michael. *Crossing the Line: Culture, Race, and Kingdom.* Spring, Texas: Illumination Publishers, 2017.

Camp, Lee. Mere *Discipleship.* Grand Rapids, Michigan: Brazos Press, an Imprint of Baker Books, 2006.

Claiborne, Shane and Chris Haw. *Jesus for President.* Grand Rapids, Michigan: Zondervan, 2000.

Jones, Thomas A. *In Search of a City: An Autobiographical Look at a Remarkable but Controversial Movement.* Spring Hill, Tennessee: Discipleship Publications International, 2007.

Roth, John D. *Choosing Against War.* Intercourse, Pennsylvania: Good Books, 2002.

Russell, Stephen. *Overcoming Evil God's Way.* Guy Mills, Pennsylvania: Faith Builders Resource Group, 2008.

Sprinkle, Preston. *Fight: The Christian Case for Nonviolence.* Colorado Springs, Colorado: David C. Cook, 2016.

Stassen, Glen H. and David Gushee, *Kingdom Ethics: Following Jesus in Contemporary Context*. Downers Grove, Illinois: InterVarsity Press, 2003.

Taylor, Dean. *A Change of Allegiance*. Ephrata, Pennsylvania: Radical Reformation Books, 2008.

Verduin, Leonard. *The Anatomy of a Hybrid*. Grand Rapids, Michigan: William B Eerdmans Publishers, 1976.

Yoder, John Howard. *The Politics of Jesus*. Grand Rapids Michigan: William B Eerdmans Publishing, 1974.

York, Tripp and Justin Barringer, editors. *A Faith Not Worth Fighting For: Addressing Commonly Asked Questions about Christian Nonviolence*. Eugene, Oregon: Cascade Books, an Imprint of Wipf and Stock Publishers, 2012.

The Kingdom of God

Volume 1 and 2

Available at www.ipibooks.com

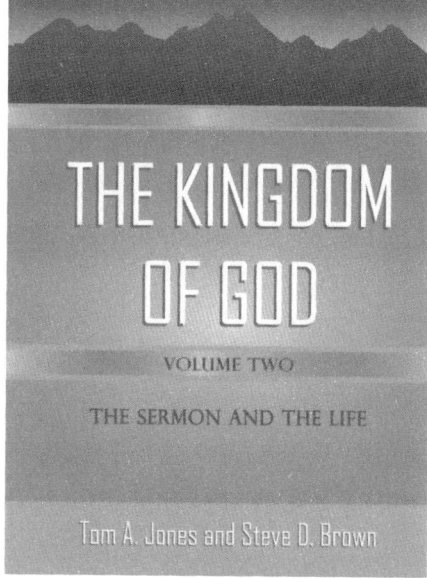

www.ipibooks.com